WE ALL DIE - HEALTHCARE INSIDERS PULL NO PUNCHES ON OUR FAILED SYSTEM

First edition. May 26, 2025.

ISBN: 979-8231964642

Written by Bela Biro and Jim Cunningham.

Table of Contents

ABOUT THE AUTHORS....1
Introduction....3
Chapter One: Dying....9
Chapter Two: How Did We Get Here?....23
Chapter Three: An Honorable Endeavor?....39
Chapter Four: Physicians....53
Chapter Five: Say "Maybe" to Drugs....65
Chapter Six: Eight Things Insurance Companies Whisper Under Their Breath....73
Chapter Seven: All Things Being Equal: They Aren't....85
Chapter Eight: A System empowered to say "No"....103
Chapter Nine: It's Not All Their Fault....109
Chapter Ten: Anecdotes and Observations....115
Chapter Eleven: Designing a Better System....127
Epilogue....135

WE ALL DIE

HEALTHCARE INSIDERS PULL NO PUNCHES ON OUR FAILED SYSTEM

Bela Biro

&

Jim Cunningham

ABOUT THE AUTHORS

Bela Biro

It's a wonder that Bela Biro can even write nearly two decades after sustaining a potentially life-threatening closed-head brain injury. He used his head to break the fall from the garage loft onto the concrete floor below. Within five minutes of the accident, 911 was called, and a full rescue operation was initiated. First responders initially feared the worst, with some predicting potential blindness, at best. However, thanks to the swift actions of the emergency team, the expertise of top neurologists and other physicians, unwavering support from family and friends, access to advanced trauma and medical services, and consistent follow-up therapies, the only lasting consequences are 83% hearing loss in the left ear and occasional bouts of vertigo. He considers himself incredibly fortunate.

From an early career in public accounting, Biro transitioned into a finance role with a publicly traded HMO as the organizations were just coming up. The time saw these new organizations mostly as an opportunity to reduce healthcare premiums for large employers, to better manage health, offset by limited choice and accompanied by very serious and appropriate criticisms for denying access to medically necessary care.

Biro continued his career in top executive roles at major medical systems, multi-specialty clinics, and health plans, always focusing on population health, healthcare leadership and innovation, and with a fervent approach to improving health outcomes and quality at lower cost. By most standards, an incredibly rewarding career. In addition to the expected rewards of high-level corporate positions, Biro experienced the heartache and frustration of a broken system, having firsthand attempted to work through the challenges while at the same time witnessing the closed-door conversations and decisions that work against a viable and sustainable healthcare system.

Today, Biro pursues a variety of personal interests, including culinary arts, writing, travel, jazz and blues bass guitar, observational astronomy, and timepiece repair and restoration.

Jim Cunningham

Inspired to follow a non-traditional career path, Jim has led, advised, and navigated many of the domains considered to be inside the U.S. healthcare system. It all began after completing his undergraduate degree at Indiana-Purdue University in Fort Wayne, where he managed a data center for a local hospital. From there, Jim went on to take on business operations, technology, consulting, and strategy roles for hospitals, growing hospital-employed medical groups, a large health insurer, a major academic institution, and an academic medical center and school. Jim returned to the front lines of healthcare by leading a large network of primary care clinics in Seattle, Washington, which is where he and Bela's paths first crossed.

Jim has developed a passion for serving the underserved, especially those suffering from addiction. He currently serves as Care Community Leader and Vice President at Indigenous Pact PBC, where he now works toward the company's mission to achieve health equity within a generation for the Native American and Alaska Native populations. In this role, Jim leads a network of clinics treating people suffering from opioid addiction.

In his spare time, Jim enjoys writing on the topic of leadership and providing leadership coaching. He lives in Seattle, Washington, and is a father of four sons.

Introduction

Figure 1: UnitedHealthcare Executive, Brian Thompson was gunned down in a suspected targeted attack in Midtown Manhattan

Figure 2: Protestors reflect the public grievance in support of murder suspect Luigi Mangione

With overlapping and complementary executive-level healthcare careers, we have collaborated on some chapters and co-authored others, drawing upon our extensive real-world experience, anecdotes, and a rare breadth of insights across all segments of the industry. This book highlights numerous aspects of the broken U.S. healthcare system and calls for immediate action.

Is it possible to rethink a system that works for *all* of society versus the current approach? This book is not only a peek behind the curtains at what regularly occurs across the United States in an incredibly complex and dysfunctional healthcare system, but also a cry for collective thinking and action to effect radical and immediate change to our often-failed delivery of healthcare.

The current system is failing too many Americans. The pain, suffering, mortality, and economic costs are simply too high. While small — and even some significant and important — changes are in the works, there is no question that a complete do-over is in order. The time and opportunity for meaningful, immediate change and long-term overhaul is *now*.

The writing of this book follows the heinous daytime fatal shooting of a UnitedHealth Group top executive—an act attributed to frustrations with our healthcare system. Even the comedy team at *Saturday Night Live* used the event to provoke an ironic laugh, explaining that the American public's reaction to the shooting was, "Yeah, well, healthcare stinks." The company's CEO, Andrew Witty, subsequently stated publicly that the U.S. healthcare system "is not perfect" and that coverage decisions "are not well understood." In a guest essay in *The New York Times*, Witty wrote, "We know the health system does not work as well as it should, and we understand people's frustrations with it. No one would design a system like the one we have. And no one did. It's a patchwork built over decades."

Healthcare in the U.S. is sadly — and undeniably — a massive business. However, it stands apart from all other industries in these startling ways:

> **Unpredictable Access:** Consumers (patients) lack certainty about service availability and delivery timelines.
>
> **Opaque Pricing:** Patients are unaware of upfront costs and their ultimate financial responsibility.
>
> **Inflated Charges and Uncertain Payment:** Providers bill significantly more than they anticipate receiving, with reimbursements varying wildly depending on the insurer — or the "self-insured" consumer. Providers can only use sophisticated models to estimate what they will ultimately be paid in aggregate.

Ranging from medical miracles on one hand to greed, corruption, mismanagement, poor access, mistakes, malpractice, profits, scandals, high costs, and even pandemics on the other, U.S. healthcare is currently ranked **69th** in the world. That's the recent ranking by the Legatum Institute, a London-based think tank, based on their global evaluation of where to find the best healthcare. Singapore ranks first, with countries such as Uruguay, Kuwait, Poland, Iran, Turkey, and many others ranking ahead of the United States.

Another renowned organization, the Commonwealth Fund, recently reported the U.S. as ranking **last** for performance among the healthcare systems of eleven (11) high-income countries — **despite** spending far more of its gross domestic product (GDP) on healthcare. Their analysis was based on 71 performance measures across five domains: access to care, care process, administrative efficiency, equity, and health outcomes. Among the countries evaluated, Norway, the Netherlands, and Australia ranked at the top.

And then there are these statistics:

> **Life expectancy** in 2021 was **six (6) years shorter** in the U.S. than in peer countries (76.4 years in the U.S. vs. 82.3 years on average in comparable countries).
>
> **Children and teens** in the U.S. are less likely to reach adulthood compared to their counterparts in peer nations, with significantly higher rates of motor vehicle accidents, firearm deaths, and suicide.
>
> The U.S. is a glaring outlier with the **highest rate of pregnancy-related deaths—23.8 deaths per 100,000 live births** in 2020—compared to **3.6 deaths per 100,000** in similar countries.
>
> As of 2022, U.S. **national health expenditures** made up **17.3%** of its GDP—the highest health spending share among developed countries.

If the intent is to provide reliable, high-quality, competitive, and affordable healthcare, the current United States "system" fails. Rather, the existing system is perfectly designed to achieve the unimpressive outcomes and exorbitant costs it delivers.

To be clear, that system includes a convoluted insurance landscape made up of government-run, publicly traded, privately held, and not-for-profit institutions — not to mention the increasingly common "no-offering" option, with many people lacking any healthcare coverage whatsoever. Insurance aside, the actual delivery of healthcare itself is disparate and uncoordinated, spanning everything from behemoth multi-state hospital systems to academic medical institutions, from varied medical and administrative staff models to solo local provider offices. The accompanying business and ownership structures are equally wide-ranging and often lack any objective rationale beyond income generation and tax avoidance.

These entities further diverge in orientation—ranging from faith-based to secular—with a host of other biases embedded within those frameworks.

It's often said that our system is "broken," even in the face of real and remarkable advances — be it life-saving medications or innovative procedures with successful outcomes. We submit that something must first be working well to later be described as "broken." The truth is more sobering: the system isn't merely broken — it was never whole to begin with. And that becomes clear in the many real exchanges and stories shared from the high-level underbelly of the nation's healthcare quagmire.

Chapter One: Dying

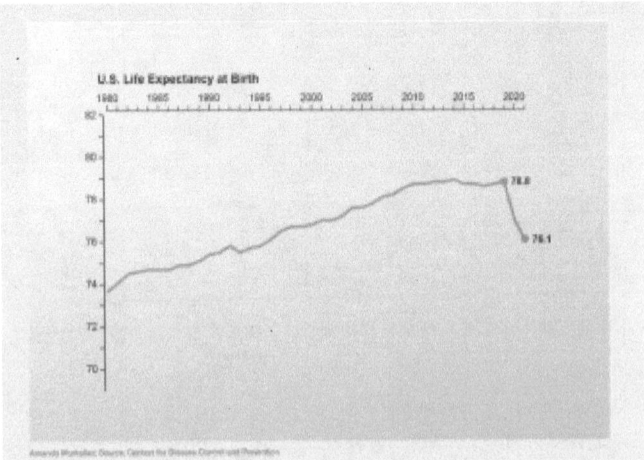

Figure 3: COVID-19, drug overdoses, and death from firearms have set the U.S. life expectancy back decades, but the experience of dying in our dysfunctional system is perhaps the most tragic part of the story.

We all know that death is inevitable. Nevertheless, it remains a largely taboo subject in the United States — often avoided due to a complex interplay of stigma, deeply ingrained and varying religious beliefs, and a pervasive fear of mortality. Unlike in the U.S., many cultures have developed elaborate rituals and social structures to embrace death more openly and respectfully. Our immediate neighbor to the south, Mexico, celebrates the Day of the Dead, honoring deceased loved ones with food and festivities, maintaining a connection with ancestors. In many African cultures, the passing of a loved one is marked with ornate celebrations featuring music and dancing, both honoring the deceased and supporting grieving families. Tibetan and Buddhist cultures often leave the deceased body exposed for a natural return to the earth—symbolizing the cycle of life and death.

A contemporary expert on the subject, Sherman Solomon — a university professor, author, and sought-after speaker — regularly states that we in the U.S. are the ultimate death-denying culture. In fact, he may have coined the term. We rarely acknowledge this because, well... any such acknowledgment would contradict the very notion that we are, indeed, the ultimate death-denying culture. Our avoidance of the topic manifests in many ways, such as the widespread procrastination of estate planning — including the creation of wills and documented end-of-life advance directives.

This last point is where the U.S. healthcare system comes into play, often making matters worse. The complexities and high costs of the American healthcare system frequently exacerbate the emotional and financial burden on individuals and their families, making the end-of-life process even more traumatic and devastating.

The following personal anecdote poignantly illustrates the multifaceted challenges and systemic failures inherent in our deeply flawed healthcare system — particularly regarding end-of-life care:

Dad

It was early 1988, and my (Bela) father's family had gathered at my parents' Southern California home to celebrate his 50th birthday. Growing up, outward expressions of love weren't common in our household. We rarely, if ever, said "I love you," though the feeling was certainly there. It just wasn't something we voiced. Even so, it felt natural to include "I love you" in my birthday toast. In some strange twist of fate, that may have been the first time I'd ever said those words to him aloud. And it would be the last.

Just a week later, my mother called before dawn — long before my alarm clock went off. My father was in the hospital — ironically, at the same hospital where he had worked for years in the lab as the chief medical technologist. He'd suffered arrhythmia or heart attack in his sleep. My mother had woken to a painful sound, found him unresponsive, and called 911. He was admitted to the ICU, intubated, monitored, and tested — all while remaining in a coma. The hospital stay, with my father, entirely unresponsive, lasted nearly a week.

This was the late 1980s, a time when documented advance directives were practically unheard of. Families were often left to make life-or-death decisions. Knowing that my father had been deprived of oxygen for an extended period and noting his minimal brain activity, he was only being kept alive by machines. My mother faced a dreaded choice. She and my father had discussed their wishes over the years, and they both knew where they stood. The decision was clear, and my mother bravely conveyed their will to the doctors — many of whom were close family friends. It was what Dad wanted. A kind, intelligent man — a MENSA member (an international society whose sole qualification for membership is a score in the top 2 percent of the general population on a standardized intelligence test" — he wouldn't have wanted to continue with a compromised existence.

Dying in his sleep, beside my mother, spared him a long and painful illness. Even the week in the ICU, though agonizing, was mercifully brief — tougher on us than on him. It was a stark and difficult week, yes, but a short chapter in the larger story of his life. In our current U.S. healthcare system — where prolonged illness can be both physically and financially devastating — his passing, while heartbreaking, avoided a potentially far worse scenario; he was spared prolonged suffering. And in a system that so often mishandles end-of-life care, that offers a small measure of comfort. It doesn't erase the pain of losing him, but it softens the edges, allowing me to remember him not for his final days, but for the kind, intelligent, and loving man he was.

Jerry

I spent as much time as I could with my close friend Jerry after his pancreatic cancer diagnosis. He was 67 years old, living alone in a Puget Sound-view condominium north of Seattle, with friends and family residing nearby. I had connected him with specialty physicians and joined him at several appointments, including a lengthy consultation with a surgeon scheduled to perform a complex procedure — Whipple surgery.

Also known as pancreaticoduodenectomy, the Whipple procedure involves the removal of multiple parts of the digestive system, including the head of the pancreas, the first part of the small intestine (duodenum), the gallbladder, and the bile duct. New "plumbing" is then constructed to redirect the functions of these removed parts. It's an overwhelming procedure by any measure.

The surgery was scheduled, but once the surgeon opened him up, it became clear the cancer had already spread—to the bladder and surrounding areas, many of which showed visible cancerous spots. Rather than complicate things further, the surgeon made the call to close Jerry up without completing the procedure.

I was with Jerry shortly after he was wheeled back to his room from recovery. He had just learned that the procedure hadn't worked out. He was disappointed, and mostly just wanted to know what would happen next — and how much time he had left.

Over the next day, several physicians visited him. Jerry asked each of them the same question: "How much time do I have?" But he kept getting passed around. The hospitalist suggested he speak with the oncologist. The medical oncologist deferred to the radiation oncologist. A resident had no idea. Finally, the surgeon who had attempted the operation responded directly. With an apparently heavy heart, she told him: "Six to twelve months."

Jerry, always the optimist, figured he really had a good shot at six to twelve years. He pursued radiation and other treatments over the following months. But as it turns out, there's really no such thing as early detection when it comes to pancreatic cancer. His decline was rapid. In the end, his last days came closer to the six-month mark.

Jerry spent his final months living with his daughter and son-in-law. They adapted their spare bedroom with a hospital bed and his personal belongings to make him as comfortable as possible. The family provided daily care with immense love and devotion — but without the benefit of nursing education, clinical experience, or the physical and emotional stamina needed for 24/7 caregiving.

Their support spanned everything: pain management, help with bathing, dressing, and meals, and the emotional burden of witnessing Jerry's rapid decline. One particularly late evening, Jerry fell while trying to get to the bathroom. He hit his head on the floor and required a trip to the emergency room for stitches.

The ER physician, familiar with Jerry's case, offered an option: admission to the hospital's hospice unit. This was notable — dedicated inpatient hospice units within hospitals are rare. More commonly, hospitals provide "comfort care" within general wards, a kind of workaround. Another typical alternative is discharge to a Skilled Nursing Facility (SNF), though the quality of these facilities can vary dramatically depending on location, cost, and management.

After careful consideration, Jerry and his family chose to admit him to the inpatient hospice unit. They were grateful for the break from providing round-the-clock care and the chance to focus on quality time. At this point in his illness, it was expected he would stay for three to five days—possibly longer—to manage acute symptoms and receive "respite" care.

I visited Jerry as often as I could during his time in the unit. We talked a lot about death, as the end became more apparent. One of his later quotes has stayed with me: "Dying is not at the top of my list of things to do, but it's OK."

Another moment I often shared came when I asked if he remembered the project we worked on together years earlier when we were at the same company. He said, "No, I don't remember." I replied, "Me neither." Then he added, "Nobody does."

It was a quiet, powerful message about what really matters.

Jerry's passing was quiet, without pain, and allowed friends and family to visit and say their goodbyes. It also spared his family the added burden of monitoring medications, not knowing what to expect, and simply waiting.

Fast forward several years—the hospital announced the permanent closure of its 16-bed inpatient hospice unit, explaining that actual demand for care had never met projections, even though the unit had served more than 2,000 patients over nearly seven years of operations.

Seriously? The more honest explanation likely lies in this: the unit, when evaluated on a standalone basis, never made money. In its best year, it somehow *lost* $2 million.

Joan

My mother-in-law, Joan, raised five kids as a single parent, worked a variety of jobs, failed retirement because she kept going back to work, and even helped care for her own mother, who passed away at 103. Later in life, she was diagnosed with breast cancer — and beat it.

Then came regular checkups. Only a few years later, the cancer returned. This time, it had metastasized, affecting her bones. The cancer was systemic.

Joan lived on a small, fixed income—Social Security. It wasn't enough to cover her cancer medications, let alone everyday expenses like food. She never talked about the pain, but I knew. Day in and day out, she endured a lot. Some days, she couldn't lift or move her arms without excruciating pain. Cooking meals? Impossible.

Around the same time as this latest diagnosis, her life partner of many years passed away. Then came chemo, radiation, and countless visits to physicians and treatments at the hospital near our home—far from where she lived, especially with traffic being the norm, not the exception.

Joan came to stay with us for several months to be closer to her treatment. We helped her with daily living, and despite the constant pain and grim outlook, she remained positive. She reflected often on her life — her accomplishments, her family, her gratitude. Our conversations were deep and meaningful, covering everything from cherished memories and family stories to her thoughts on the afterlife. These moments felt sacred — though not necessarily in a religious sense.

In her final weeks or months, Joan moved to her son's home—a quieter and more comfortable environment—where she received home hospice care. Unfortunately, this is where things began to unravel. Not because of Joan's condition, but because of the care.

We quickly learned that not all hospice services are created equal. In fact, they vary dramatically. Joan needed more comprehensive support, particularly for pain management. The first provider explicitly outlined their limited services and minimal visits—clearly failing to tailor care to her needs.

Her family scrambled to find a replacement. After researching and interviewing several options, they ultimately switched to a more reputable home hospice organization. It seemed promising. And it was... just OK. Until her final hours.

The memory of those last hours will haunt us — her surviving children and the rest of her family — for the rest of our lives.

For reasons that remain a mystery to this day, the hospice provider would not (or could not) administer intravenous (IV) pain medications at home. Joan couldn't take oral meds at that point, so crushing pills and placing them under her tongue while she cried in pain was both inexcusable and profoundly undignified.

After Joan's passing, the hospice nurses left. Her family was left alone waiting for the transport service. Watching her body zipped into a bag and lifted vertically out of the home was another traumatic moment we will never forget.

Joan's passing is just one example of the stark inconsistencies in hospice care across the United States. Despite the indignity of her final moments, her legacy lives on — in her children, grandchildren, and great-grandchildren, and in the hearts of all who were touched by her remarkable journey.

Dana

Dana was 79 years old. She presented as highly intelligent and well-read, with a thick Italian accent that remained strong despite having lived in the United States for over six decades and pursuing higher education here. She reportedly followed a vegetable-rich, healthy Mediterranean diet and appeared physically fit. However, she was a lifelong heavy smoker and consistently avoided physicians and medical advice — despite her husband's career as a hospital clinician.

One day, Dana called her son, who lived in an adjoining state, about a four-hour drive from her Southern California home, to tell him she had called an ambulance to take her to the hospital. After months of doctor's visits with little to no follow-up — including delayed or nonexistent return calls — and, finally, excruciating and intolerable pain in her esophagus; she could no longer bear it and decided to be admitted.

Her son and grandson immediately drove to California to be with her. They found her in the ER, with IVs, still in pain. A doctor had examined her, but more information was forthcoming. The situation seemed grim. Unfortunately, this was only the beginning. The coming weeks would be much worse, marked by a complete lack of diagnosis or misdiagnoses, limited access to coordinated care, and a constant rotation of physicians.

That hospitalization, the first of several, lasted five nights and included various imaging studies and pain medications. Unexpectedly, the focus was primarily on cardiac issues rather than the esophageal pain that had prompted her admission. Dana had previously described a minor heart attack several years earlier but had never pursued follow-up care. She consistently denied the need for self-care, refused to quit smoking, and possibly struggled with severe depression — regularly expressing a desire for her life to end.

Her discharge from the Southern California hospital included a prescription regimen for cardiac issues, requiring medications to be taken every few hours — but still no diagnosis for the severe throat and neck pain that continued to plague her. These unresolved issues would lead to repeated hospitalizations and re-admissions over the following weeks.

Dana's son and daughter-in-law moved into her home to provide 24/7 care, navigating a revolving door of hospital stays and returns. With no clinical training or outside support, they struggled to meet her increasingly complex needs. Amidst the chaos, they also helped Dana address her long-postponed estate planning by connecting her with an attorney. And they honored her wish to explore the recently enacted California End of Life Option Act — commonly referred to as "death with dignity" — working tirelessly to help her understand and pursue the option if she chose.

They advocated aggressively, but the challenges proved insurmountable. The law required a definitive terminal diagnosis and the ability to self-administer the prescribed life-ending medication. A confirmed diagnosis remained elusive — physicians were either unable or unwilling to document the multiple suspected advanced-stage cancers. And Dana's debilitating throat and neck issues rendered swallowing — even small amounts of food or water — nearly impossible.

As an alternative, a hospice physician recommended in-home hospice care, with her son administering increasingly aggressive doses of opioid pain medication. The goal was to mirror the intent of the End-of-Life Option Act: a peaceful end, with pain minimized. But for her son, the emotional weight of administering medication that could ultimately cause his mother's death was overwhelming.

In a final workaround, Dana was discharged from her last hospital stay to a Skilled Nursing Facility (SNF) for "rehabilitation." Everyone involved — the hospital and the SNF — knew rehabilitation was not a realistic goal. But this arrangement ensured the SNF would accept her and that her Medicare Advantage plan would cover the cost, sparing the hospital from incurring additional unpaid days if she remained there and passed away.

Dana was my mother.

Jim

Born in 1937, Jim enlisted in the United States Marine Corps in his late teens, prior to the U.S. deploying combat troops to Vietnam. Although he thankfully never experienced front-line active duty, his enlistment concluded with an honorable discharge, qualifying him for lifelong Veterans Affairs (VA) benefits.

Those VA healthcare benefits were later supplemented by Medicare enrollment once he became eligible. Together, these programs provided Jim with the ability to evaluate various providers, choose between VA and private facilities, and access treatment options for a range of medical issues — including multiple cancers, heart procedures, and, ultimately, head trauma resulting from repeated falls.

The head injuries began with an initial fall and were followed by additional accidents, leading to a series of medications and neurological procedures to address slow, persistent brain bleeding. As his condition grew more complex and his prognosis more uncertain, Jim was placed in an inpatient VA hospice facility in the South Puget Sound region of Washington State.

That might conjure a certain image — but the reality was quite different.

A tree-lined drive led up to the facility, which overlooked a beautiful golf course on military land. The hospice building was relatively new, part of a broader campus of Veterans Administration buildings. It was not at all what I had expected.

Jim had been a difficult personality in his younger, healthier days, and his challenges only intensified after his head injuries and hospice admission. His complaints and forgetfulness understandably escalated. Still, we witnessed the VA nursing staff — and every other staff member — treat Jim, his roommate, and all patients with kindness, compassion, and, above all, dignity.

As can be expected in a hospice setting filled with mostly elderly veterans, patients passed away frequently. In those moments, a powerful ritual took place: a United States flag was placed over the veteran's body for transport. Every staff member — whether a nurse, physician, cook, or part of the maintenance team — would stop what they were doing, line the hallways, stand at attention, and salute as the body was carried out.

Those few minutes of silence, honor, and reverence brought comfort and a deep sense of respect to everyone present. It was a stark contrast to other facilities where, all too often, staff rush in to clear a room and prepare it for the next patient as soon as someone has passed.

It's worth noting that, while the VA frequently receives negative media coverage, they do not maintain a dedicated public relations or marketing department to tell their side of the story, which makes real accounts like this one even more important to share.

These experiences with end-of-life care, though deeply personal, reflect situations where individuals and their families had both healthcare access and knowledgeable advocates. The financial and emotional trauma is often significantly greater for those who are less privileged or less informed.

The acceptable alternatives are limited. While hospice units and home hospice care aim to provide as much quality of life as possible in the final weeks or months, these services can be expensive and highly inconsistent.

For elderly individuals who qualify, Medicare will cover some hospice services — such as doctor visits, equipment, physical therapy, and short stays in hospice facilities, or for respite care. But — and this is a big but — Medicare does not cover room and board, any treatments or medications intended to cure the illness (since hospice care is focused on comfort, not curing), and definitely not emergency room visits or ambulance rides.

The stark truth is this: we often do better with our pets at the end of life than we do with our fellow humans.

When our animal companions are suffering and their quality of life has diminished, we often make the painful but compassionate decision to end their suffering through euthanasia. We tearfully prioritize their comfort in those final moments — ensuring they are surrounded by love and spared prolonged pain.

Yet when facing similar circumstances with human loved ones, we often become entangled in a complex web of medical interventions, legal obstacles, and emotional uncertainty that prolongs life well beyond the point of meaningful existence. We hesitate to talk about end-of-life wishes, as if the conversation itself is an admission of defeat. Worse still, even when those wishes are clearly expressed, they are too often ignored.

This reluctance — combined with a healthcare system heavily oriented toward aggressive, ongoing treatment — frequently results in a final life's chapter marked by discomfort, disconnection from loved ones, and the denial of the peaceful, intentional closure we so readily grant to our pets.

Surely, we can do better.

Chapter Two: How Did We Get Here?

Figure 4: Palace of Pietro Pfanner in Lucca Italy

Let's start with a visit to the Tuscan city of Lucca, Italy, a city tracing its roots to as early as the 3rd century BC, having obtained the status of a Roman colony in 180 BC.

Why Lucca? The answer lies in a tourist visit to the palace of the late Pietro Pfanner, a physician that cared for the wounded who came from the front during World War I and later became the Chief Physician of Surgery in 1918 at the hospital of Lucca. He was renowned for having cared for all classes of citizens, from the great composer Giacomo Puccini to house calls for the neediest, where he was said to have left money to buy medicine hidden under their pillows.

A tour of the palace provides a closer look at the grounds and statues of the garden that can be viewed at a modest to an even closer distance during a "passeggiata" on the Lucca wall. Staircases, fresco-covered ceilings and walls, ornate rooms — and you are finally confronted by glass cases displaying medical-surgical instruments and ancient medical texts that belonged to the physician. Most of the instruments are cold metal gynecological tools whose design and use are almost unimaginable, except for the fact that they are very visibly on display, and only a century since they served as state-of-the-art. Focusing only on one gender-neutral instrument, you will observe the "double-flow vesical catheter," allowing for irrigation of the bladder to treat urinary tract infections (UTI). Without the knowledge that they were caused by microorganisms, this treatment provided for an upper stream to flow into the bladder and to then exit through the lower part of the apparatus to be fully gathered in a basin. Much earlier catheters were described as having been made of silver, copper, brass, and horn. So, this contraption was indeed the most advanced for its time. Without the knowledge and ability to otherwise cure UTIs, reliance had otherwise been on, among other things, hospital stays, bed rest, attention to diet, and bleeding. Yes, bleeding.

The use of direct bleeding has been highlighted in movies, historical and fictional series, and books — mostly for dramatic effect — but drawing on historical reality. Indeed, bloodletting is one of the oldest medical treatments known, dating back to ancient Egyptian, Greek, and Roman cultures. The practice is believed to have peaked during the Middle Ages and Renaissance, when it was used to treat most illnesses, even extending to mental illness. Of all the bloodletting techniques, direct venesection — the act of slitting a vein open to drain blood — was perhaps the most dramatic. From royalty to commoners, not surprisingly, the results were mostly less than positive. To treat a patient suffering from a high fever, a physician would use a lancet to cut into a vein, allowing the blood to flow freely into a bowl. The loss of blood would almost certainly leave the patient weak and dizzy, but with the hope that the loss of blood would break the fever. It usually did not succeed. Combining direct bleeding with leeches was an advancement that yielded similarly unfavorable results. The use of leeches in medicine also dates to ancient Egypt, where they were applied directly to wounds to help with healing. Like direct bleeding, leech therapy reached its peak in Europe in the 19th century for a variety of conditions. Picture a patient with a swollen leg, cause unknown. A specialist in leech therapy would apply several leeches to the affected area, allowing them to suck the patient's blood. The patient would certainly feel a strange sensation, a combination of wetness and pressure. Leeches do indeed possess anticoagulant properties that can aid in the healing of wounds. However, limited knowledge and widespread application often caused more harm than good. Fortunately, the significant advancement of germ theory and better (effective) treatments emerged, with these blood-draining treatments going by the wayside — but not until well into the 19th century.

In sharp contrast, with a few examples culled from recent headlines:

Baby born at 21 weeks survives, against all odds

Born at only 21 weeks and 1 day into gestation — meaning he was about 19 weeks premature—Curtis was able to come off his ventilator at 3 months old and was discharged from the hospital at 9 months. After six months at home, Curtis and his family received a Guinness World Record certificate acknowledging him as the most premature baby in the world to survive.

Working pig kidney is successfully hooked up to a human

With human organs in short supply for transplant surgeries, scientists have long been working to make animal-to-human transplants safe, feasible, and widely available. In recent years, doctors connected a pig kidney to a human and watched as it effectively filtered waste from the body and produced urine. While still experimental, the success could signal a big step forward for animal-to-human transplants, though many questions remain.

Robotic Surgery

Robot-assisted surgery in the U.S. has become ubiquitous in the 21st century. The systems are used for procedures ranging from heart valve repair to prostatectomies and gynaecologic surgeries. Different from the limited rotation of the human hand, a robotic arm can fully articulate in all directions. The fine and full movement of the robotic arms couples perfectly with the significantly enhanced viewing through the equipment — as compared to the human eye alone — materially enhancing the opportunity for micro-precision surgeries.

A recent grand opening at a Pacific Northwest hospital, prior to any patient being admitted, provided the opportunity for visitors to view and even try their hand at the state-of-the-art device. Even untrained teenagers and young adults were given the chance to give the tools a go. These individuals have grown up in a world of computer gaming and technology, with no training on the device, no advanced degrees — armed only with their world experience and intuition. They looked through the viewer and were quickly able to grasp, move, and manipulate small objects with the complex machinery. This next generation of surgeons will encounter a medical world unimagined even a generation or two ago.

Pharmaceuticals

The pharmaceutical industry responded quickly to the COVID-19 pandemic, with two notable companies rapidly developing and gaining FDA approval for competing vaccines — and later, for prescription medications to help fight the infection in its early stages. These solutions were in sharp contrast to the multi-year research, development, clinical trials, financing, FDA approval, and marketing typically required for medications intended to address other conditions. Cancer and other disease-state medications continue to improve and increasingly show further promise. Diseases that affect smaller numbers of people garner less attention, principally due to the time, expense, research, and low projected return on investment (ROI). Sadly, and at the same time, there's no shortage of news reports regarding the industry's proliferation of opioid addiction, price gouging, lawsuits, immoral business practices, and medications that produce side effects worse than the diseases being treated.

The reader will note that these real-life medical wonderment stories involve treatment or recovery following a diagnosis or traumatic event.

Less published or apparent are the stories where a life could have been saved if only the proper steps or medical expertise were available or executed. The U.S. healthcare picture is even more bleak if we go upstream just a little way to reveal how much illness or treatment could be avoided if only the many system gaps or failures were addressed. Perhaps Artificial Intelligence capabilities will provide the advancement to avoid illness or to earlier diagnose and address treatment. The predicted resources for AI to interpret various imaging have already been well addressed, with the ability for astonishingly large volumes of data and diagnoses to be immediately, in real-time, compared to a current patient's X-ray, CT, MRI, or ultrasound imaging results. Accuracy and lower cost to produce specific tests, diagnoses, and even procedures are within the realm. However, we submit that if all the new developments existed under the current financing mechanisms, the population impact is likely to continue to fail miserably. That is, an elite class will most likely access and receive the most advanced — best care and services — while preventive care and education would not improve meaningfully. Various individuals and organizations will revise and refine the models to extract profit, the masses will still be relegated to scrambling for services, and we will fail the most desperate — even as they continue to fall victim to bankruptcy and something akin to debtor's prison through no fault of their own.

With amazing and rapid treatment advancements, and with yet more on the horizon, how is it that U.S. healthcare is near the bottom of the list? The answer lies not solely, but mostly, in how U.S. healthcare is financed — with too many players participating in the profit quagmire and with intertwined perverse incentives. Contributing factors range from heavy student loan debt for early and even later-practicing physicians, ever more pressure to schedule more patients, "full" patient panels, insurance and regulatory documentation requirements, and medical malpractice exposure — including behemoth awards and attorney fees. Executive compensation incentives are also intertwined in the system, including healthcare providers, pharmaceutical companies, insurance or payer organizations, equipment suppliers, and the many related and even ancillary services and suppliers. Very obviously, profit and greed often surpass doing what's best for the patient — all in the realm of considering time and cost to properly diagnose and treat versus the time and related compensation to provide world-class care.

Healthcare in the United States is mostly financed directly or indirectly through insurance provided through government programs including Medicare, Medicaid, and the Veterans Administration, or through private insurers (e.g., the BUCAs—Blue Cross and Blue Shield plans, United Healthcare, Cigna, Aetna—the payers). For a surprisingly high number of individuals lacking healthcare insurance coverage, self-pay is the only remaining — and often most expensive — last resort. This point is particularly ironic when considering that full payment is generally not expected for the fees charged by hospitals, physicians, emergency rooms, and most other healthcare providers. Amounts and discounts negotiated by the payers are materially lower than the sticker prices that appear on a patient invoice. The lower expected payments vary by payer and represent a complex accounting calculation for the healthcare providers, who can only estimate — rather than record with certainty — the amounts that will ultimately be paid for their various provisions of care.

Understanding that healthcare services are usually discounted, why is a healthcare list price — a "charge master" — even necessary? Who pays those exorbitant list prices? Indeed, the only consumers expected to pay the highest invoice amounts are those who can least afford it — those who are not employed and covered by a company-sponsored health insurance plan or through other government programs. Not quite a debtor's prison, but financial devastation due to full-fare medical bills is not uncommon.

Formal health insurance is a relatively recent financial structure within the United States, as pre-paid services gained popularity during the early 20th century when hospitals and physicians found themselves sharing in the financial ruin of the Great Depression. Healthcare had historically been primarily paid out-of-pocket, with individuals responsible for directly covering the costs of medical services, medications, and hospital stays. Hollywood has again highlighted the wild west days of bartering for doctor visits — with farm produce from hens and pigs to canned goods that were "put up" for the winter — in exchange for visits and treatments. While this system appears direct and simple, many people were challenged by the expense of paying their medical bills. Selling assets and depleting savings was the name of the game for many facing unexpected serious illnesses or injuries. Without any means to pay, access to healthcare was often limited or entirely denied. Some limited forms of health insurance did exist, such as fraternal benefit societies and mutual aid organizations. These groups provided mutual assistance to their members, but their coverage was often limited and not widely accessible. With the increased offerings of pre-paid healthcare, the turning point to the broader "business of healthcare" had gained full speed.

A variety of factors came together throughout the mid-20th century to accelerate the proliferation of health insurance. The chief among them was the tax treatment of employer-sponsored health plans. Having been granted tax-exempt status, it became convenient for employers to offer the appealing healthcare coverage "fringe benefit." This was especially valuable during World War II, when the only way to enhance employee compensation was through non-monetary benefits due to strict wage and price controls. The employer-provided healthcare insurance benefit ultimately synced up nicely with the labor movement's push for health insurance as a standard element of employment contracts.

The next game-changer came with the actuarial profession, which had long and deep roots analyzing volumes of data to determine life expectancy so that life insurance companies could assess and minimize financial risk while ensuring profitability. The profession quickly added healthcare analysis to their portfolio as commercial insurers pursued market dominance. Rather than life expectancy, "experience rating" was born — an ingenious approach for meticulously analyzing the historical claims data of specific employers or population groups so that health insurers could accurately assess their risk profile and adjust premiums accordingly. The approach was a win-win: health insurers' profitability was assured, while cost-conscious employers also benefited as they eagerly sought to secure the lowest-cost health insurance for their workforce. Soon, the playing field was leveled as most other insurers adopted the strategy, fostering a competitive insurance market.

With several decades of employer-sponsored healthcare coverage increasingly engrained in the U.S. workplace, a gap remained for individuals after they retired. While some employers offered a retirement health insurance program in addition to retirement plans, many retirees were left to return to the old way of paying for hospital and doctor care on their own. On average, the healthcare coverage gap wasn't expected to last long, as people didn't typically retire until well into their 60s. Life expectancy wasn't far behind — 67 years for men and several years longer, at 74, for women. The coverage shortfall was addressed in 1965 with the landmark legislation establishing Medicare to cover older Americans.

On the other hand, it took several decades for Medicare's glaring misstep of a cost-based reimbursement system to be addressed. The system was initially set up for healthcare providers to be paid based on their actual costs. With minimal incentive to closely — or even remotely — monitor expenses, medical inflation often exceeded inflation for all other goods and services — and still does.

The passage of the Employee Retirement Income Security Act (ERISA) in 1974 introduced yet another significant variable, allowing employers to tailor and price their own "self-insured" health plans. This essentially gave employers the option to compete with — or altogether eliminate the need for — commercial insurance. Employers could now assume the financial risks (and rewards) associated with providing healthcare coverage to their employees. Today, the country's largest employers, as well as many mid-sized and even smaller employers, are self-insured. Think Microsoft, Boeing, Amazon, the large automakers — all self-insured. Nevertheless, many large, self-insured employers still rely on the network discounts negotiated by, as well as the analysis, claims payment, and overall administration offered by the BUCAs (Blue Cross, United, Cigna, Aetna). Don't worry — the insurance companies are still getting their cut!

The ongoing super-inflationary health cost trend ultimately led to — or created the opportunity for — the emergence of Health Maintenance Organizations (HMOs) or managed care in the 1980s and 1990s. The more modern labels, often incorrectly applied but interchangeably used nevertheless, include managed care, value-based care, and population health. Managed cost is the real and true phrase of the day — though spoken only sotto voce — with the reality being a cost containment goal, as health plans sought innovative strategies to turn the tide, or at least to slow the trend.

Limited provider networks through selective contracting — a bold departure from traditional practices — proved to be a beacon of hope (and profit) for innovative early adopters. By establishing contracts with a limited or select network of healthcare providers who agreed to accept lower reimbursement rates in exchange for a guaranteed patient volume, managed care plans represented a new and innovative offering. New HMO companies emerged, and public stock offerings flourished, as many entrants to the market were embraced and well-rewarded by Wall Street. The new price competition among healthcare providers was alleged to force them to become more efficient and to reduce costs. Some succeeded; many — from independent providers to larger systems — failed under the new and poorly understood contracting structures.

Early resistance from the medical fraternity has waned since those early days but has not vanished by any means. The assertion continues that standardized reimbursement rates and restrictive protocols overly limit physicians' ability to charge fees commensurate with the complexity and intensity of the care they provide, not to mention the lifestyles to which they had become accustomed. HMOs argue that the lower fees for complexity and intensity are mitigated by fixed payments made to providers for patients who require little, and sometimes no, care whatsoever — as well as by adjusted fixed payments for patients with well-documented higher risk (also a lofty and complex topic).

The 1990s and 2000s were marked by consolidation of healthcare providers, along with increased public backlash against the utilization management (UM) practices employed by managed care plans. Most Americans experience and will recognize that UM practices persist, as they encounter required referrals for care, pre-authorization requirements for procedures, denials for services and claims payments, and — most of all — limited access.

Nevertheless, the bargaining power of health plans suffered due to the need to maintain adequate provider networks with the increasingly large healthcare systems that had resulted from mergers and acquisitions. Simultaneously, the utilization management practices implemented by managed care plans — aimed at controlling healthcare costs by limiting the use of certain services — faced mounting criticism from patients and providers alike.

A real-life example, presented here in a fictionalized format to preserve anonymity, captures the tension well. In a conversation between a decision-making healthcare executive (co-author) and a physician executive within the same organization, the exchange went something like this:

MD: You know, 30% of medical procedures are unnecessary.

Exec: Yes, I sure do understand that many surgical procedures are not necessarily in the patient's best interest.

MD: The reason I bring this up is because I've been reviewing your statistics. And I see that your unit is only denying 18% of the pre-authorization surgical procedure requests.

Exec: Yes, that's correct. That's been our average "denial rate" for some time now.

MD: Well, that leaves a lot of unnecessary procedures being performed and paid for by us.

Exec: Actually, our Utilization Management team of nurses and physician medical directors have reviewed all the requests for pre-authorization. All the requests that have been approved have been deemed medically necessary. You're not asking me to direct the team to deny more claims even though they are medically necessary, are you?

MD: No, no. That's not what I am saying at all! But it's often easy to find a way to justify the procedures using various criteria or even using the individual's judgement to approve the procedures. And there is a big gap between 18% and 30%. You should talk to your team!

Exec: I see. I'll investigate the matter (dismissing the MD executive)

Seriously, where did this 30% figure come from? Is this a widely accepted statistic for all medical-surgical procedures? Was this an internally derived value? Most likely, is this a statistic conveniently promoted internally by this insurance company's top leadership? Be assured — these conversations happen within insurance companies regularly.

These developments — a perfect storm of adverse factors — undermined the full ability of managed care plans to effectively negotiate lower prices with healthcare providers, further exacerbating the challenges faced by the healthcare system.

Consumer-driven health plans gained traction in the mid-2000s, reducing some of the insurance risk borne by health plans as they shifted much of the risk burden to the consumers of healthcare. These innovative plans, a departure from traditional insurance models, combined never-before-seen high-deductible insurance with tax-sheltered health spending accounts. By shifting a greater portion of healthcare costs to consumers, these plans aimed to incentivize individuals to make more informed decisions about their healthcare spending. The tax incentives offered for saving money in health spending accounts provided an added motivation for consumers to take a more proactive role in managing their healthcare expenses.

The Patient Protection and Affordable Care Act of 2010, often referred to as "Obamacare," marked the most recent significant shift in American healthcare history — resulting from many years of debate and deliberation, not to mention politics. Even at that, many argue that the Act was written and rushed without enough thorough evaluation to consider all aspects of what can easily be described as the most complex healthcare system in the world. It markedly addressed some real shortfalls but made some matters worse.

The Act introduced a mandate requiring individuals to purchase health insurance and expanded Medicaid coverage for low-income adults, with the goal of increasing the number of Americans with health insurance coverage and reducing the number of uninsured individuals. While many parts of this significant, complex, and multifaceted piece of legislation were — and continue to be — evaluated and debated, the Affordable Care Act unquestionably sought to address the systemic challenges plaguing the healthcare system and to ensure that all Americans had access to affordable, quality healthcare.

At the forefront of the evaluation and debate: Did it work? Was it a significant improvement, or just a little bit? What exactly are the measurable gains? And what are the unintended and negative impacts? We are now at a point where we are left only with healthcare financing options to explore, including: the status quo, Medicare for All, a single-payer system, concierge physician practices, abandonment altogether of employer-provided health insurance, individual allowances for the purchase of care, systems modeled after those in other countries, and wilder ideas yet.

The headline resistance to the notion of a single-payer system is rooted in concerns that taxes required to fund the system would be too high, that healthcare would be overutilized if readily accessible as a societal benefit, and from physicians and hospitals — again — that they would not be adequately compensated.

The argument that there isn't enough money to adequately provide healthcare for the population of the most powerful and wealthiest country in the world falls flat when considering that health expenditures are already approaching 20% of the country's GDP. In fact, over one-third of the U.S. population is already covered under government programs including Medicare, Medicaid, and military-related healthcare benefits. Just under two-thirds of the population continue to be covered by employment-based insurance or direct-purchase coverage.

Many remain uninsured — even though they may qualify for Medicaid or other government programs — often simply because they are unaware that they qualify, or that the coverage is available to them.

Notably, and sadly, the real risk to broad offering and acceptance of government-provided healthcare for the entire population may simply depend on who is in the top office of the land.

Chapter Three: An Honorable Endeavor?

Figure 5: Steward Healthcare CEO Dr. Ralph de la Torre was paid out $250m over four years.

Figure 6 Healthcare CEO Ralph de la Torre made $250m and enjoyed a lavish lifestyle while his hospital chain (Steward healthcare) collapsed.

Honorable, "Deserving of respect or high regard", Merriam-Webster Dictionary

Keeping our fellow citizens healthy and ensuring they have access to life-saving care when they fall ill, or are injured, is an honorable thing to do. To be sure, our country is blessed with hard-working professionals of all sorts who got into their chosen medical field for all the right, and arguably altruistic, reasons. The question that should be asked is, are the executive leaders in the industry just as honorable as the endeavor they lead and the professionals, we all depend on? The answer is that many are not.

Of course, our finger-wag at leadership is a generalization that involves a fair amount of self-reflection, but it does represent the rule and not the exception. The underlying reasons for such a deficit in leadership are only surprising because we think of our local hospitals, doctors, and maybe even our employer's Blue Cross medical plans as a shield of protection for ourselves and our families, just like the local fire department. These traditional views of healthcare are no longer reality, and maybe never were.

Depending on how long you've been around, or in the community where you live, you may remember a time when your local hospital was independently operated or operated as part of a local or regional organization. There is a good chance it may have been, maybe still claims to be, non-secular; anchored by the values of an organized religion. Most of these "systems" were, and remain, non-profit, but they have also consolidated with other hospital-based organizations into much larger businesses. You've probably seen a name change, or new branding and logos. You may have also noticed that those same hospital-based organizations began taking over physician practices and perhaps your own doctor has joined a conglomerate. What does this have to do with leadership? In short, it is about ambition, greed, mismanagement, and misinformation. Let us explain.

Be they for-profit or non-profit, there is no difference when it comes to the career ambitions of healthcare senior-level executives. There are many ways to get to the top, and unfortunately few relate directly to the performance of the organization. CEOs tend to overstate their commitment to an altruistic mission, while simultaneously cutting resources away from patient care and redirecting it to pet projects, physician demands, innovation spin-offs, and acquisitions or mergers. CEOs that remain with small communities or rural critical access hospitals that have not become part of a multi-state conglomerate tend to earn much less than their large health system counterparts while performing better. It is in the CEO's personal interest to champion growth through consolidation because the bigger the organization the higher their salary; again, performance be damned. The public talking points behind all of the consolidations usually cite it as an opportunity to lower costs and improve quality, neither of which has happened. There was a time when this was a plausible hypothesis, but the evidence is in and those continuing to champion large healthcare conglomerations are doing so to benefit their own economic circumstances and career ambitions, not because the health outcomes will be any better.

Like other industries, healthcare executive pay has been on the rise and, as stated, there seems to be less and less direct correlation between organizational performance and CEO pay. It is worth noting that as many as two-thirds of hospitals and 60% of health insurers remain in a not-for-profit status and, in that regard, their CEOs far out-earn leaders of other non-profit sectors. Why, with such an honorable endeavor as healthcare, are CEO salaries looking more like those of publicly traded companies and less like someone who leads a non-profit foundation?

In an excerpt from an April 2023 REAL CHANGE NEWS article titled, **Health care companies cry poverty but pay big salaries to execs,** John Burbank writes...

Nonprofit hospitals also enjoy lucrative tax exemptions.

"Providence avoids more than $1 billion a year in taxes. In exchange, the Internal Revenue Service requires them to provide services, such as free care for the poor," according to the New York Times. But in 2020, Providence spent less than 1 percent of its expenses on charity care.

Perhaps the worst hypocrisy is how these hospitals, crying wolf, are paying their chief executives. Keep in mind that these are tax-exempt institutions; it is odd that they behave like profit-maximizing centers.

This only makes sense in the words of Dr. Rod Hochman, Providence's chief executive: "'Nonprofit healthcare' is a misnomer. It's tax-exempt healthcare. It still makes profits."

Hochman is leading the charge for profits and benefitting along the way. His salary soared from $4.1 million in 2016 to $11.5 million in 2017.

Hochman is a big wheel, but he has a lot of company in our state. Brian Ivie, CEO of Skagit Valley Hospital, received $1.1 million in 2021. Jeff Tomlin of Evergreen Health in Kirkland received more than $1 million. The top three executives at Kaiser received more than $5 million combined. In Vancouver, the CEO of the Salmon Creek Hospital made $1.8 million.

MultiCare Health System, which received more than $280 million in federal coronavirus money just in 2021, paid its top three executives more than $6 million. Overlake in Bellevue paid its CEO more than $1.5 million. PeaceHealth Hospitals in Bellingham and Vancouver paid two executives more than $1.2 million each. Virginia Mason, which received $51 *million in coronavirus money in August 2021, paid one officer $3.5 million and another $2.4 million.*

And let's not forget the children: Seattle Children's Hospital received $79 million in COVID-19 payments in 2021 and paid its CEO and another executive more than $1.4 million, plus $1.1 million to a third executive.

Most healthcare executive leaders, even those who may have started with honorable intentions, end up chasing after professional and financial success through a number of strategies. Here are just a few:

Clever branding is an art and is often used as camouflage to disguise a bad product or service. Back in the early 2000s, a charismatic young hospital CEO named Quint Studer started a crusade to improve the patient's experience. Many of Mr. Studer's tactics were effective and continue today, using survey data from patients as a foundation for improving service and prioritizing resources in a hospital. Studer quickly created less of a culture and more of a cult by mastering the manipulation of the Press-Ganey survey process, training nurses and other staff members how to "encourage" patients before being discharged to complete the survey.

As you can imagine, when you are ready to leave the hospital, if the only thing standing between you and going home is checking a few boxes, then how much thought and energy will you put into providing real feedback that is constructive, yet critical? When the caregiver is in the room, it almost ensures high marks. Under those early years of the Studer phenomenon, this translated into large banners branding his hospital as ranking in the top 1% by Press-Ganey. Studer went on to form the Studer Group (purchased since by Huron for $325 million), a national consultancy company built to spread its evangelical message to a lot of eager clients paying handsomely to help Studer cover the cost of his private plane and build great personal wealth.

Was care improved by the work of Studer and his enthusiastic followers? It is likely that the perception of services improved, and it certainly inspired a movement to place the experience at the center of many healthcare operations, but in the end, it was about branding, big money, and leadership ego. Today, CEOs build a brand through logos, clever taglines, and creating a branded culture — none of which are supported with the resources necessary to deliver a product equal to the promise of the brand. If we are going to improve the delivery of healthcare in our broken system, we must end the practice of building brand in lieu of product and focus on actual health outcomes performance.

While this book outlines a healthcare system turned Frankenstein by decades of confused policymaking, overregulation, greed, political divisions, and perverse stakeholder incentives, we believe even a poor system can function better with the right leadership. There are leaders in the industry who have maintained a true north, working to improve quality and access while lowering costs, but those examples are in the minority. Don't be fooled by the rhetoric of CEOs and their marketing teams who successfully build a brand but not a sustainable and high-performing organization. The reality of what drives decision-making in most healthcare organizations is not a reflection of their masterful branding, but instead a reflection of choosing careerism over the honorable endeavor.

CEOs and other healthcare leaders will often talk about how "healthcare is local," yet that is largely a myth. You might go to your local emergency room, hospital, or doctor, but decisions about how they work, how they are paid, and how they are organized are rarely made locally. Standardization of services is prized by executive leaders who want to create a Starbucks-like common experience no matter where services are delivered. Most often, standardization of people, processes, and technology are valued much more than outcomes. Just a quick look at some of the largest health systems by KFF — an independent source for health policy research, polling, and news — makes our case for healthcare being anything but local, and anything but non-profit.

"Provider markets have become increasingly consolidated over the past 30 years. Following a wave of consolidation in the early- and mid-1990s, there were 1,573 hospital mergers[1] from 1998 to 2017 and another 428 hospital and health system mergers[2] announced from 2018 to 2023. The share of community hospitals that are part of a larger health system also increased from 53% in 2005 to 68% in 2022 (see Figure 1). Relatedly, the share of physicians working for a hospital or in a practice owned at least partially by a hospital or health system increased from[3] 29% in 2012 to 41% in 2022."

---

1. *https://www.aha.org/system/files/media/file/2022/11/2018-TrendWatch-Chartbook-Full.pdf*
2. *https://www.kaufmanhall.com/insights/research-report/2023-hospital-and-health-system-ma-review*
3. *https://www.ama-assn.org/system/files/2022-prp-practice-arrangement.pdf*

System Name	Hospital Beds in 2022	FY 2023 Operating Revenue	Ownership	States with System Hospitals
AdventHealth	8,038	$16.8B	Nonprofit	*9 states* CO, FL, GA, IL, KS, KY, NC, TX, WI
Advocate Health*	10,528	$28.2B	Nonprofit	*6 states* AL, GA, IL, NC, SC, WI
Ascension Health	16,241	$28.3B	Nonprofit	*13 states* AL, CT, FL, IL, IN, KS, MD, MI, NY, OK, TN, TX, WI
CommonSpirit Health	17,148	$34.5B	Nonprofit	*18 states* AR, AZ, CA, CO, GA, IA KS, KY, MN, ND, NE, NV, OH, OR, SD, TN, TX, WA
Community Health Systems	9,850	$12.5B	For profit	*16 states* AK, AL, AR, AZ, FL, GA, IN, MO, MS, NC, NM, OK, PA, TN, TX, WV
HCA Healthcare	38,015	$65.0B	For profit	*19 states* AK, CA, CO, FL, GA, ID, IN, KS, KY, LA, MO, NC, NH, NV, SC, TN, TX, UT, VA
Kaiser Permanente	9,217	$100.8B	Nonprofit	*3 states* CA, HI, OR
Providence	9,445	$28.7B	Nonprofit	*7 states* AK, CA, MT, NM, OR, TX, WA
Tenet Healthcare	12,822	$20.5B	For profit	*12 states* AL, AZ, CA, FL, MA, MI, OK, PA, SC, SD, TN, TX
Trinity Health	14,621	$21.6B	Nonprofit	*17 states* CA, CT, DE, FL, GA, IA, ID, IL, IN, MA, MD, MI, NJ, NY, OH, OR, PA

More recently, we are seeing some new players get into the healthcare fray. On one hand, given that healthcare accounts for nearly one-fifth of the U.S. Gross Domestic Product (higher than any other developed nation), it is understandable that growth-oriented, entrepreneurial types would want to get in on some of the action. But on the other hand, the size of the pie is already too large, and more takers seem only to increase its size.

Not surprisingly, Amazon entered the market in a big way by acquiring the boutique primary care chain *One Medical* in February 2023. Offered as a discounted subscription to Prime members, Amazon hopes to broaden access to care that more traditional healthcare entities have been unable to deliver on. Amazon is not alone, as CVS, Walgreens, and Walmart are all getting into the mix, too. Amazon paid

$4 billion for One Medical and topping that investment — around the same time — was CVS purchasing Oak Street Health for a whopping $10.6 billion.

While Oak Street grew rapidly, touting their value-based approach, they still operated at a loss, expecting to lose over $200 million in 2023. In a November 2023 NPR article and interview[4] with Forbes Contributor, Bruce Japsen, host Ayesha Rascoe ended with a pointed question.

> *RASCOE: Well, I mean, as we're talking about this, I mean, we're talking about this because these are businesses. They are looking at the bottom line. What happens if they can't turn a satisfying profit in health care?*

> *JAPSEN: Yeah, you're seeing that now. I think that these entities close stores all the time. You know, if there's a neighborhood where there's a store that's underperforming, they will close them. And, you know, they have great intentions, but they will hopefully be very careful when they open these stores and move into markets where they think they can be a success because if they're not, and the community starts to use them but maybe not as much as Walgreens and CVS and company want, there could be a situation where they would pull out.*

There are a lot of ways in which the new players may be gambling away billions of dollars, not the least of which is that they don't really understand the incentives inside the industry, how consumers perceive quality, and the short supply and burnout of the people delivering the care. There is an arrogance on the part of these large corporations that, because they have thrived in a rational retail marketplace, they can

4. https://www.npr.org/2023/11/12/1212534782/amazon-is-getting-into-health-care-will-it-actually-make-care-more-accessible

apply the same concepts in healthcare and solve all sorts of problems those before them have failed to solve. Time will, of course, tell, but make no mistake about it — between the large consolidations of companies and the entry of new players, healthcare is anything but local; it is big business and run by very top-down conglomerations that make decisions about how we all get our healthcare.

Punctuated by the adaptations made during the COVID-19 pandemic, technology has — and will — play a big role in transforming how healthcare is delivered. Many changes are welcome and can impact actual clinical care or access for those who otherwise may not be able to get the care they need. Health-tech company start-ups have sprouted up but are sometimes more weed than flower. The jargon of "transformative," "innovative," and "seamless" is for branding — but not so much an accurate description of the experience. Leaders are naïve about what barriers remain and make outlandish claims about what their venture capital-backed solutions can do.

One CEO for a merged tech and primary care company liked to say, "we are solving the affordability crisis in healthcare." Not only was that not true, but it was a new level of either naïveté or arrogance. Another CEO for an addiction recovery start-up company liked to fly around the country speaking at conferences and boasting about the success of their company's proven business model. After continued losses and not meeting investor expectations, they were asked to step down. This was after much of the company had been laid off and services scaled back. Today, the company is continuing to cut down and back out of markets — likely to sell or unwind the venture.

We want to be clear: advances in information and clinical technology have a significant place in healthcare, and we do not downplay those opportunities. That said, we will not tech-our-way out of this broken system, and leaders in the industry need to understand that.

Enthusiastic technovators jump right into an industry in much need of help, only to be faced with a complex regulatory landscape, strict privacy and security requirements, a challenging set of stakeholders with limited resources who are less likely to adopt unproven solutions, and a very fragmented and siloed industry that makes integration akin to finding compatible parts that will work for both a 2024 Polestar EV and a 1955 Chevy Bel Air.

Technovators can lead improvements in the healthcare industry, but many will underestimate the hurdles and fail. Depending on what source you lean on, health-tech start-up failure rates range between 65%–90%, and yet there is little slowing down their enthusiasm with "transformative" ideas. In our broken system, technology plays a role if those directing its development really understand the problem they are trying to solve. If we design a new system for delivering care, technology can become the foundation upon which real leaders will improve quality and outcomes while lowering costs. That said, it can't be stressed enough: access, affordability, and quality outcomes are not guaranteed by technology alone. A new healthcare system design that is enhanced with technology is our only real way out.

Of course, nothing has more influence on the industry than money. *Opensecrets.org* broke down lobbying efforts based on data from the ***Center for Responsive Politics***, which was sourced by the Senate Office of Public Records. Accordingly, they found the following ranking of money spent on special interest groups. Topping this list was Pharmaceuticals/Health Products, which spent $5.8 billion from 1998 to 2023—outpacing all other industries. They also cite,

> *The pharmaceutical/health industry is also a top spender in political campaigns, with contributions reaching a total of $89.09 million in 2020. This was a 170% increase from a decade earlier. The industry's top lobbying priorities over the past few years included:*
>
> - *Opposition to H.R. 3 (a bill allowing the government to negotiate and cap drug prices, which served as a blueprint for*

drug pricing provisions in the Inflation Reduction Act)

- *The COVID-19 vaccination effort*
- *Resisting government-run healthcare*

Coming second was Insurance (includes health property and auto), spending $3.6 Billion over the same period of time.

> *The insurance industry includes the health, property, and auto insurance companies along with agents and brokers. It has historically mounted a lobbying effort second only to that of drugmakers and other healthcare product providers.*
>
> *From 1998 to 2023, the insurance industry spent nearly $3.6 billion on lobbying. Health insurance companies[5] have occasionally fought over healthcare legislation against drugmakers, hospitals, and other healthcare providers, with each group blaming others for fast-rising costs. In 2023, Blue Cross/Blue Shield[6] led industry lobbying efforts with spending of $20 million. It was followed by America's Health Insurance Plans with $13 million in outlays.*
>
> *In the 2020 election cycle, individuals and political action committees (PACs) aligned with the insurance industry made a total of $120 million in contributions to federal political campaigns. In early 2022, that health insurers' group opposed legislation cracking down on the industry's frequent rejections of mental health and addiction treatment claims.*
>
> *More contributions from the insurance industry have gone to Republicans than Democrats in every election cycle since 1992.*

---

5. *https://www.investopedia.com/the-best-affordable-health-insurance-companies-4782687*

6. *https://www.investopedia.com/blue-cross-blue-shield-medicare-review-5118467*

It comes as no surprise to most of us that our nation's system of sick care is a by-product of a free-market approach poisoned by a political environment vulnerable to satisfying those with dollars to spend instead of the actual consumer of services. While things like the Affordable Care Act (Obamacare) and, more recently, the Inflation Reduction Act accomplished certain things — such as broadening access to coverage and lowering drug costs — these were incremental accomplishments offset by more complexity and regulation.

These incremental changes are evolutionary, not revolutionary, and our system needs a revolution if we expect to compete with the rest of the world in how we safeguard the health of our citizenry. You can't have a revolution without leadership, and part of a revolutionary retooling of our healthcare system will require new leadership that is high-integrity, community-minded, and up for the honorable endeavor of healthcare.

Chapter Four: Physicians

Figure 7: The Agnew Clinic by Thomas Eakins

Core to much of our healthcare system are the most highly trained professionals who engage in our care... physicians. I (Jim) began working with physicians in the mid-1990s as an administrator of a small, growing primary care group and have worked closely with them almost ever since. Because I consider so many physicians friends and have enjoyed getting to know and work with them, it is difficult to be critical of them knowing they are largely a product of the same broken system we want to see overhauled. There is also a lot of good to be said about the profession that should be acknowledged and appreciated.

Why is understanding the physician community an important part of this story? Physicians play a critical role in leading organizations, research and innovation, and often coordinate the care delivered by their teams to diagnose and treat us when we are ill. We can't consider the many aspects of our broken system without giving voice to those that can make the diagnosis and healing of a plethora of diseases and injuries possible.

You will be spared much of the tortured history of how medical practitioners have evolved since the early times of our forefathers but we want to give enough context to level-set a general understanding. Ben Franklin — yes, that Ben Franklin — in addition to his legendary status as a founding father of our country, he also was a founder of the modern-day university system. In 1751, he helped found the first hospital, and we've never been the same since. During my work at the University of Pennsylvania, I was fortunate enough to have an office in the John Morgan School of Medicine Building, constructed in 1904. My office had one large, curved marble wall because it was juxtaposed to what had been part of an observation theatre where students watched surgeons perform their craft. Interestingly, in more modern times, the building had to have restrooms retrofitted for women; the original architects hadn't envisioned a world where women would study medicine just as their male counterparts. Today, we have nearly 425,000 female physicians and a 1.6 -1 male-to-female ratio.

Times have changed, and in this respect, we are all better off because of it.

History aside, in our country, to become a physician is a thing of honor and prestige. Any parent is proud when their child is accepted and heads off to medical school. The large houses that grace the best neighborhoods in our towns are, many times, those of physicians, and when we make a trip to our local hospital, the convenient, dedicated parking space for physicians is full of shiny, top-of-the-line cars. As young people aspire to a career in medicine, they envision a good and affluent life; they imagine all the hard work and self-sacrifice they make for years and years of training beyond their undergraduate work will pay off in spades.

Medical schools rarely prepare them for what that career is like in our healthcare system. They don't tell those interested in family medicine or pediatrics that the burnout rate is high, the compensation is not what they may have expected, and that patient care would be time-limited to optimize the revenue necessary to cover their salaries and the care team staff supporting them. The American Medical Association reports that for 2023, almost half of all practicing physicians reported experiencing at least one symptom of burnout. This is truly a matter of flawed expectations and assumptions about this strained and hierarchical profession.

In reality, the system is hierarchical because physicians' income varies drastically by specialty, where neurosurgeons and other sub-specialties are financially deemed at the top of the M.D. food chain, and internal medicine, family medicine, and pediatrics are considered necessary, nearest the bottom of the physician compensation pyramid. The variation can be measured in multiples of up to well over one hundred (100x) for specialty neurosurgeons compared to Primary Care Physicians (PCPs). Before concluding that "that's not fair," let's remind ourselves that pay for work in the U.S. is not based on a system of meritocracy, but rather what one can get for her/his labor or profession.

Furthermore, let's not feel too sorry for the lowly primary care physician (PCP). Physician incomes, including PCPs, are well ahead of those for most families in the U.S., and well ahead of similar specialties in other countries. Nevertheless, the flawed expectations and realities of burnout are real factors that require consideration for a functioning healthcare delivery system.

Medical schools don't tell subspecialty trainees — be they in cardiology, neurology, or many others — that they will become siloed in their respective areas of interest and exacerbate a system that lacks coordination of care and fosters parochial behaviors between specialties. Depending on the supply of any given specialty, they may be able to leverage their expertise for a higher salary, but a focus on prevention is a luxury they can't afford, and volume is king. Many new physicians at the beginning of their careers expect that the payoff begins on day one and that building a practice or paying more dues is not a barrier to instantly buying that large house, expensive car, or family boat. Instead, they find themselves barely into practice, living paycheck to paycheck, never really having been taught the economics of their career choice.

Shortly after accepting my first role to lead the operation of a primary care group owned by a hospital system, one of my first moves was to meet with the physician who would be my medical counterpart and someone I would need a collaborative relationship with. Thinking back on it now, it must have really pissed him off that his employer had decided to pair him up with a complete rookie in the world of group medical practice. I'll avoid names to protect the innocent and call him Dr. D, but my administrative assistant arranged for us to meet at a restaurant near his clinic where he was always given his regular table.

I'd heard he was a good doctor, but a tough customer when it came to partnering with administrative types. He had built a successful family medicine and occupational medicine practice before eventually selling it and getting away from the shrinking margins of primary care. He was especially well regarded by some specialties, such as orthopedics, because of his diagnostic skills prior to referring patients for more specialized treatments.

As I came into the restaurant and made my way to the back corner where his table was, I saw apprehension on his face and estimated his age was not much older than myself. He stood politely and shook my hand, and as I sat down, he looked directly at me and said, "You are fucked." Not what I expected. What more could I do but smile, listen, and learn?

Almost immediately into the conversation, he told me that physicians only care about three things: their patients, their call group, and their money. While that seemed pretty absolute, I learned that he — and many other physicians I would meet — were not ones to dabble in gray areas. Things were either black or they were white... even when they clearly were not.

Maybe we got off to a shaky start, but Dr. D and I became close friends and have remained in contact as years and jobs changed. Understanding those three priorities became a foundation for me in working with doctors. While they may be less literal than Dr. D intended, they were a guidepost that served me well. Let me expand on each.

Most — and I emphasize most, not all — physicians truly care about their patients. They are caught in a system of sick care that rations their time to the point that providing holistic care with attention to physical and mental health is simply not a practical reality. They are rushed through a day of compressed schedules, increasing requirements for documentation, managing risk of liability, adapting to changing technology, and frequently, working with support teams that experience burnout, high turnover rates and inadequate training.

On the one hand, they wish they could spend the time they need to give the best care to everyone. On the other hand, they need to do what is necessary to earn their desired salary.

Compensation is a big deal to physicians; bigger than most people realize. Physicians are competitive and, for some reason, have concluded that things must be fair, and if they "work harder" than their physician colleagues (however that is defined), they should make more money. That has set the stage for salary and incentive plans that unfortunately create perverse incentives that physicians must leverage to optimize their income. The available levers are not always associated with behavior that is best for the people they serve, but to optimize company and individual incomes.

For example, while this has been changing slightly and slowing, many physicians are essentially rewarded for the number of people they see. Once they accept these formulas, they become like hamsters on a hamster wheel, coming into the office each day and cranking through another full schedule of patients.

Recently, I visited my own family doctor for a check-up. She was about 40 minutes late. When she came in, she made a polite apology. I asked her how many patients "they" have her seeing these days. She smiled, knowing I am an insider, and said, "Most days twenty-two, but they double-booked me this morning." This is the physician hamster wheel. It is easy for administrative folks to shrug it off and say, "Well, but they make a lot of money." But my response to healthcare administrators is to ask them to imagine their own job — and what if they arrived daily and conducted twenty-two meetings in which they were responsible for creating the agenda and taking minutes? What if they did those five days a week with no end in sight? How long would they stay in their job? Hence, physician burnout and a supply problem of qualified physicians.

Physicians bear some responsibility because they often put income over work-life balance and discount — or fail to appreciate — the abysmal economic realities of healthcare... especially primary care. In one hospital-based system, I was involved in facilitating a physician compensation committee where they had a seat at the table in designing their own compensation plan and incentives. Of course, there were guardrails around what could and could not be done legally and economically, but as I would sit and listen to their discussion, all I could think about was: What would their patients think of them if they could hear this conversation? What would they think of their priorities?

I had one of those director's chairs with the canvas backs ordered with the word "patient" printed on the back of the seat. I brought the chair to a committee meeting and placed it squarely at the end of a conference table. My message was simple: let's design something that does not conflict with serving our patients, and something they might be proud to know you advocated for.

I don't imagine it made a lot of difference to some of the physicians, but I learned after I left the organization that it had an impact on some of them. One sent me a kind note telling me that he went home and told his wife that it was the damn administrator who seemed to care more about the patients than the doctors did. I think we all cared, but this system sets us up to do the wrong things, and we all get caught up in it.

Dr. D's third priority was his call group. For him, that was the example — but what it really stood for was control. In Dr. D's case and in those times, physicians had a say in who they shared after-hours call with. Why was that important? Physicians practice differently and can attract different types of patients; they can also be more or less flexible when it comes to managing schedules in a collaborative way.

For example, in those days, a group of five or six physicians might share "call" and work extremely well together, agreeing to holiday and weekend coverage in a fair way. Maybe this group is also good at prescribing and not writing too many prescriptions for pain medication. An administrator like me comes along and says we just purchased another physician practice, and he or she will be in your call group; those were fighting words. It upset the balance of the group and, more importantly, took control away.

Call groups are less of a thing these days, but loss of control is not.

One of the last bastions of control physicians have been forced to give up is their schedule. Not so long ago, if I went into a clinic where the schedulers sit, I could find Post-it notes and cheat sheets all over, telling them the individual scheduling preferences of the group of physicians they supported. This allowed an individual physician to specify things like which days they were going to see new patients and which days they started at one time vs. another. It worked fine in private practice, but when they became part of a large medical group and scheduling had to become centralized, it was no longer possible to keep up with all the exceptions. So, physicians generally practice based on scheduling templates that are administratively beneficial — not physician, or patient-centered. These are examples of the loss of control physicians have experienced while being placed on the hamster wheel.

You can't really understand physicians without having some insight into their training. There is a lot to be said about the length and degree of difficulty when it comes to what turns a high school or college graduate into a physician, and I'll give you some of those numbers at the end of this writing. What we want you to come away with is a different way of looking at how we produce physicians in this country — and why that may be a part of this broken system that deserves some attention.

Having spent a little time in the academic medicine environment, I have had numerous discussions with people over the years about their academic and training experiences and gained some insights when it comes to common misperceptions.

Many of us might like to think that physicians arise as young people with ideological visions of putting those big brains they were gifted with to use doing good and saving lives. That is certainly true in some cases, but if I had to guess (which I am), it is the exception and not the rule. Those who enter the medical field do so for all sorts of reasons. Some do it because of the prestige and expected lifestyle mentioned earlier. Some do so because it is a family legacy and expectation, they feel obligated to fulfill. Some do it because they are interested in science, and it becomes an avenue to study what interests them most. There are other reasons, but genuine motivation of the kind we all like to believe inspires doctors rarely comes into play when deciding who is most suitable for medical school.

Someone once told me that I needed to think about the medical school student or resident in training differently than I had been. They were admitted to a program because of academic excellence, and the programs that admit them don't want to see them fail — because that reflects poorly on their selection process. Those of us who thought programs weeded out the unqualified by pushing them through a rigorous and intensive curriculum that only the best could survive — as if it were the Navy SEALs — are mistaken. It may have once been the case, but it isn't now.

My colleague went on to encourage me to think about the trainee making rounds in the hospital alongside their residency brothers and sisters, and how the mediocre trainees might linger near the back, hoping not to be called on by their instructor while making rounds... just stay under the radar and get through the program. He asked me if that was the doctor, I wanted to take care of me or my family. Would I even know if my doctor was just that trainee?

Our current medical training is focused on moving people through the programs — not ensuring that only the right people suited for the work ahead succeed.

A knowledge of science, anatomy, physiology, pharmacology, etc., is important. But what about emotional intelligence? Do we teach would-be physicians how to be self-aware or how to be active listeners? Not really. Do we help them understand the full range of socio-economic determinants of health? Maybe some programs breach the surface of the topic. Do trainees understand what to expect when they enter practice, or after a few years are they going to be entering Master's in Business and Public Health programs in hopes of limiting their clinical practice and stepping into a physician executive role? Many do exactly that.

The cost of medical school is yet another consideration that must be factored into the physician mindset, reflecting a conflict between providing the best care for patients and personal income. Medical school in the U.S. is an expensive proposition — much more expensive than an international one, even if the education itself is comparable. And we are not saying it is just a bit more expensive; it is a lot more expensive. Studying medicine in internationally respected schools in European countries — including Sweden and Germany (and others) — will cost a fraction of what it takes to attend private or even public universities in the U.S.

Some justify the expense by arguing that our medical schools crank out better doctors than other countries. The argument simply doesn't hold up, with research results, patient outcomes, patient satisfaction, and a variety of objective measures proving otherwise.

The solution to the high cost of years of undergraduate university education, medical school, and foregone income while in school — followed by low-income residency — is seeking and accepting student loans bearing high interest rates.

The reality of debt financing for physicians is underscored by the real story of a practicing physician, a shareholder of a large and prestigious physician-owned multi-specialty group. Governed by its owner physicians, the M.D., specializing in family medicine, brought glasses and bottles of champagne to an evening meeting of the group's Board of Directors. As alcoholic beverages were not the norm at these meetings, the conversation quickly turned to other board members asking, "What's going on?" "What are we celebrating?" and "Who's retiring?"

As the champagne cork was popped, the doctor — a senior member of the board — revealed the purpose of the celebration: she had finally made her last loan payment. She'd made the final payment on her student loans (plural), as well as the obligatory loan to purchase shares of ownership in the medical group.

How could it be that she was just now paying off her debts — this respected, seasoned, highly regarded, nearing-retirement, hardworking physician with a very full panel of patients? The other peers and younger physicians knowingly and simultaneously cheered and sighed, in many cases with the realization that their celebration was years away.

Medicine is not an easy vocation, and my bias has often been to side with physicians. They are smart people who love to solve problems — but we can do better in figuring out who can best serve the end purpose of prevention and healing. We can do better by preparing them for what lies ahead. And physicians must own a part of their own circumstances. Greed and lost focus over what we really want to achieve falls at their feet too. Practicing medicine needs to become an honorable profession — performed by well-motivated people, emotionally intelligent people, and those who can help us change our broken system rather than perpetuate it.

Many aspiring professionals leave high school, go on to college, and get a bachelor's degree — and maybe a master's degree. Physicians finish undergraduate school and go on to spend four years in medical school and then a residency training program. According to Medical School Insiders, these are the average lengths of residency programs:

Residency Specialty	Residency Length
General Surgery	5 Years
Genetics and Genomics	3 Years
Internal Medicine	3 Years
Internal Medicine Pediatrics	4 Years
Interventional Radiology	6 Years
Neurosurgery	7 Years
Neurology	4 Years
Nuclear Medicine	4 Years
Obstetrics and Gynecology	4 Years
Ophthalmology	4 Years
Orthopedic Surgery	5 Years
Osteopathic Neuromusculoskeletal Medicine	3 Years
Otolaryngology	5 Years
Pathology	4 Years
Pediatrics	3 Years
Plastic Surgery	6 Years
Preventive Medicine	3 Years
Psychiatry	4 Years
Radiation Oncology	5 Years
Thoracic Surgery	6-7 Years

Residency Specialty	Residency Length
Anesthesiology	4 Years
Child Neurology	5 Years
Dermatology	4 Years
Diagnostic Radiology	5 Years
Emergency Medicine	3-4 Years
Family Medicine	3 Years

Urology	5 Years
Vascular Surgery	5 Years

Chapter Five: Say "Maybe" to Drugs

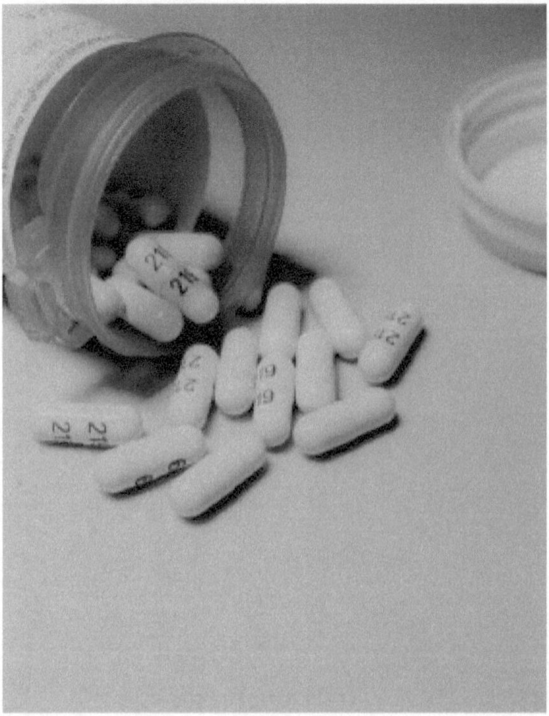

Insiders, whether on the insurance company "dark side" or on the "noble side" of providing direct care to their patients, have all but given up on fighting the Goliath in the U.S. healthcare debacle: Big Pharma. Spending on prescription drug ads now totals nearly $10 billion a year, with the decades-long marketing campaigns outstandingly successful. We are all well-conditioned to the ads with the catchy jingles, funny Rx names that seem to be missing necessary vowels, and side effects and contraindications that most notably often include death. There was a time when we would learn about prescription drugs from our doctors and pharmacists. Then came the late 20th century, when the FDA allowed pharmaceutical companies to advertise prescription drugs directly to consumers — as long as both benefits and risks were accurately represented. Thus, the low audio volume and small print at the end of most commercials.

Physicians are regularly frustrated with patients requesting specific brand-name prescription medications for what ails them — having bought into the benefits advertised and paying less attention to the small-print side effects and contraindications. Sadly, those same patients are less than willing to hear about different solutions for their condition, or even generic alternatives to the brand-name drugs they're requesting. Late for their next appointment, a full patient waiting room, and pressed for quota production, the prescribing provider often acquiesces and writes the prescription for the requested expensive brand-name drug, possibly not even the best remedy for the patient's condition.

With the number of drugs available and virtually no way of determining the current price, most prescribing physicians are not even aware of the cost of the medication to the patient. For that matter, they are surely not informed of the cost to the insurance company — which may or may not control the cost in some meaningful way through fixed formularies or, increasingly, through ownership of Pharmacy Benefit Management (PBM) companies. PBMs are the middlemen that manage prescription drug benefits between health insurance companies, pharmacies, and pharmaceutical manufacturers.

That is not to blame the providers, as drug pricing remains opaque — or carefully disguised — at best. The preponderance of prescribed brand-name medications continues the downward spiral, increasing demand and generating profits that better enable pharmaceutical companies to fund additional marketing campaigns. To be sure, keep in mind that escalating drug prices in the U.S. tend to be higher than in any other country for the same medication. With the introduction of new medications and monopoly pricing, the healthcare spending that goes to pharmacies has increased to close to one-quarter (25%) of total healthcare spending in the U.S.

Formulating and releasing new drugs is an increasingly mad scramble akin to the Klondike Gold Rush of the late 19th century. The record profits are warranted, according to the drug companies, who argue that for every 25,000 compounds that start in the laboratory, only twenty-five are tested in humans. Of those, only five will make it to market, and only one will recoup what was invested... so they explain. But that one drug; if they can just hit the mother-load, will more than make up for all the rest.

As insiders, while frustrated or even angry with Big Pharma, the allure of participation in the rush is palpable. We hear about "opportunities" all the time. An executive has a friend or relative working in pharma, or they've heard about this or that new drug coming out in some industry publication. Some small or start-up companies are working on a new wonder-drug that will cure a specific cancer. They're going to be entering trials in the coming year, not yet publicly traded, and they're seeking investors.

With no additional information — and without the need to be scientists or employees of the start-up — we can participate in the boom by simply investing from the sidelines and hoping to reap a multiple hundred percent return on our investment, enjoying the rewards in only a few short years. We won't have to work in our day jobs any longer.

However, some medications with long-standing availability and significant patient demand lack even minimal recent research and development investment. Pricing, patent protection and lack of alternatives all serve to create monopolies. The high costs associated with these medications are often unjustified and driven by other factors.

Most of us are aware of the insulin monopoly and of price gouging practices. Insulin is but one high-demand, well-known, and necessary medication for the treatment of diabetes. High prescription drug prices for insulin — and many even more exorbitantly expensive medications — are achieved by the fact that treatments for serious diseases are not nice-to-have items but are needed by helpless patients who seek to improve quality of life or prolong it. A high price is not a barrier.

On this point alone, physicians frequently encounter patient questions about improving their risk from disease or surgical complications. For instance, a patient diagnosed with a healthy heart, despite a 1–2% risk of heart disease, will often inquire about strategies to further reduce that risk. Similarly, a patient facing minimally invasive hernia repair will seek information not only on the extreme question of surgical survival rates, but also on the likelihood of adverse side effects. We humans will pay anything to better our chances when a physician confronts us with the provided estimates. For serious diseases, patients and their families are willing to pay any price to save or prolong life.

Then there's the gamesmanship of stalling generics, or the reality of a drug becoming obsolete by the time the patents expire, and generics can be prescribed.

The U.S. healthcare debacle cannot avoid reviewing the role the pharmaceutical industry has played in accelerating the opioid crisis in the United States — or, for that matter, worldwide. The addictive potential of opioids like OxyContin was initially and continuously minimized. Instead, their safety and efficacy for chronic pain management were touted. Aggressive marketing campaigns by companies like Purdue Pharma succeeded in deceptively convincing many physicians to overprescribe opioids, leading to widespread addiction and deaths from overdose.

A board-certified physician specializing in the care of critically ill patients in the intensive care unit (ICU) at an affluent Pacific Northwest area hospital explained that a quarter (25%) of his practice would be eliminated through resolution of the opioid crisis. While it is only one physician's estimate in a single city's prosperous community, extrapolating that figure across the U.S. population can only be described as staggering.

While physicians have been undoubtedly complicit in the crisis, they have also faced significant limitations in their ability to effectively treat addicted patients. The X-waiver — a federal requirement for physicians to obtain a special license to prescribe Suboxone, a medication-assisted treatment for opioid addiction — created significant barriers to access. This burdensome regulation limited the number of physicians who could treat opioid addiction, leaving countless patients without appropriate or adequate care. Physicians were limited to treating thirty (30) patients in the first year of prescribing, increasing to 100 after completing additional training. The government finally removed this restrictive barrier in response to the overwhelmingly obvious detrimental impact of the X-waiver.

Furthermore, some pharmaceutical companies have faced legal consequences for their role in the crisis. Lawsuits filed by states and municipalities have resulted in substantial settlements, holding these companies accountable for their deceptive marketing practices and the devastating consequences of their actions.

These efforts nevertheless remain insufficient to fully address the ongoing addiction crisis. While some companies have faced repercussions, many others have escaped scot-free. The long-term impact of these settlements is up in the air, and the crisis continues to devastate communities across the country and worldwide.

Perhaps the most challenging matter is the lobbying power of the industry. While lobbying efforts span across all healthcare sectors, it is appropriate to segregate Big Pharma's influence. Individual pharmaceutical companies and their trade organizations spend hundreds of millions of dollars in lobbying annually, typically outspending all other industries in their efforts.

Despite those efforts, we can take solace and hold onto some hope — and some positive forward momentum — with relief afforded by passage of the Inflation Reduction Act of 2022. The legislation, signed into law in August 2022, allows Medicare to negotiate some prescription drug prices and caps out-of-pocket spending for Medicare beneficiaries.

Ultimately, the core issue lies in the argument that pharmaceutical companies will cease developing vital new medications without profits attributable to the ability to charge excessive prices to offset the immense costs of research and development — including projects that never make it to market.

Billionaire entrepreneur Mark Cuban's entry into the market with Cost Plus Drugs serves as a visible counterargument to this assertion. Cuban has openly discussed the company's strategy of price transparency and reasonable margins at scale. He has further criticized the healthcare system's inefficiencies and expressed his intent to reduce consumer costs. By eliminating traditional middlemen and offering significantly lower prices, his company is sure to generate profits, increase his net worth, and simultaneously exert a positive influence on drug pricing for consumers.

However, while price transparency itself may be significantly impactful, it's not enough. The more complete answer to this huge and distinct segment of the industry may require more global coordination, including:

Patent reform, including fixed duration of patent protection starting with first approval and prohibiting additional patents on approved drugs that seek to increase patent life

Penalties for pay-for-delay schemes and frivolous lawsuits that delay generic or biosimilar entry

Expedite approval processes for generic drugs, that is, drugs proven to be identical to the brand name drug as well, and for biosimilars that are not exact copies of the brand name drug, but with the same active ingredient.

Regulatory reform, including deceptive marketing practices

In the meantime, as patients and consumers, we can appreciate and lean on the unsung saviors in the sector... pharmacists. Doctors in their own right, pharmacists are highly educated professionals, having earned a Doctor of Pharmacy (PharmD) degree. They are so much more than technicians simply filling prescriptions and they play a crucial role in patient care by explaining how medications work to treat specific conditions, addressing patient concerns, and offering alternative treatment options or strategies to enhance medication effectiveness.

The pharmacist is often the individual who is most critical in providing medication reconciliation, a vital step that helps prevent medication errors by identifying and resolving discrepancies in medication lists from various prescribers and across different healthcare settings.

When all other resources fail, talk to your pharmacist!

Chapter Six: Eight Things Insurance Companies Whisper Under Their Breath

Figure 8: The Buffalo Bills stadium's naming rights are paid for by Highmark Blue Cross Blue Shield, which entered into an initial 10-year agreement with the Bills on March 29, 202. Highmark is one of thirty-three Blue Cross Blue Shield Plans in the U.S..

Whisper Number 1 - "Your long-term health isn't worth our investment today."
(But we want you to get your flu shot)
The news media has helped to bolster the term "wellness" in recent years. And, the healthcare insurance industry is right there, marketing their offerings for employee wellness programs they've designed and sponsored to the point that many larger employers offer wellness programs as a benefit to their employees. That's worth repeating, even if only here in writing. Wellness is now marketed or believed to be a benefit!
Are wellness and long-term health synonymous? Do the wellness marketing efforts infer that insurers really want you to be well, or going even further, to live long, happy, and healthy lives?
With a focus on short-term profits, annual executive bonuses, and most notably, expected "churn" (employers periodically change health insurance carriers and employee turnover is now the norm as individuals are regularly forced or opt to change jobs), the apparent answer is a resounding "no." Very simply, there is limited monetary incentive for insurance companies to care about how healthy you may be several years from now. After all, you probably will be in a different job, in a different geographic location, and insured by a competitor insurer. The investment in your long-term health now is not likely to reap long-term financial rewards for the company. Even worse, the investment today will more than likely benefit another insurer once they've picked up your coverage as a relatively medically and mentally healthy person, with no chronic illness, well-adjusted, spiritually content, socially gratified, and least likely to access the healthcare system at all — or at worst, at materially lower cost than the many of us that could take better care of ourselves.
What about that flu shot? The insurance company sees a different dynamic with the shot. Annual national health expenditures for flu-like symptoms and illnesses are consistently measured in many billions of

dollars. Add the cumulative cost of millions of lost working days and the economic burden multiplies, seemingly exponentially. For the insurance company that pays for the flu shots at costs that amount to something less than a rounding error, the short-term (next quarter earnings, the favorable impact to this year's executive bonus plan), the ROI is astounding.

Whisper Number 2 – "We don't like to think of our customers as people"

Insurers much prefer thinking in terms of "member" or enrollee. After all, doesn't everybody want to be a member? And PMPM (Per Member Per Month) rolls so much easier off the tongue than PPPM (Per PERSON Per Month). You see, thinking of the insured members as actual people that are living their lives and need quick care and responses to their healthcare needs is a burden that insurers simply would rather not have to acknowledge. Insurance member benefits are specific and limited, just like for members at any club or other membership organization. It's easier for insurance company decision makers and even for their employees to sleep well at night with a clear conscience than to realize that they are dealing with real people for whom the policy will not cover a life-saving procedure, that the person's needed medication won't be paid by the insurance company because it is too new, that the individual's diagnosis requires an insurance company medical panel review, or simply that the policy for the desperate individual is limited in total dollar amount of healthcare benefit or that the person's employer selected a policy based on price versus comprehensive coverage for the individual or family.

Whisper Number 3 - "We care about operating profits, but NOT that much".

This whisper appears to be the most counterintuitive in the face of publicly traded earnings releases and executive incentive plans based on profitability. However, in the long run, insurance companies do just fine with cumulative small margins or even break-even profits from insurance operations.

Insurers may experience small or even larger losses in some years, but they almost always offset those with profitable years in the long haul. You will hear insurers crying wolf over this quarter or that year's profits from insurance operations. Yet, they know they can survive underwriting cycles and turn those losses around in future periods through pricing strategies, ever-changing insurance product designs, and strict utilization management, to name a few. No matter what, the company's net worth will continue to grow due to investment portfolios that have been well documented to perform well over the course of the companies' lifetimes.

The question arises as to how these companies have access to funds for investment in the face of cumulatively small or even non-existent margins from their insurance operations. The answer lies in the fundamental cash flow structure for all types of insurance. Simply put, premiums are billed and received in advance or very close to coverage effective dates, while outgoing claims are paid slowly, over a much longer period—this is known as insurance float.

Investing money that builds over time, even with razor-thin margins, is a significant contributor to the insurers' bottom line. However, you will hear a cry of panic when their portfolios decline due to market crashes, such as the 2008 plunge related to the Financial Crisis and the 2020 dive following the start of the COVID pandemic.

Whisper Number 4 – "We hate new pharmaceutical wonder drugs!"

Wondrous developments are indeed delivered by the pharmaceutical industry—ranging from weight loss to erectile dysfunction to the latest breast cancer regimens. The ads for wonder drugs for many chronic and even never-before-heard-of conditions are seemingly endless. Not all, but most—or at least many—of the prescription medications work as intended and advertised, notwithstanding the endless list of possible side effects. When effective, the drugs improve and even extend lives and reduce the need for other medical interventions. It can be argued that some medications will lower the cost of care... in the long run!

So, why in the world would the healthcare insurance industry hate the new wonder drugs? Simply, new drugs are often most expensive when initially released and during the early patent years, and the insurers will not have had adequate lead time for their underwriting and actuarial teams to model the costs and long-term benefits of the new drugs.

To that last point about the long-term benefit of the new drugs, the issue goes back to Whisper Number One: "Your long-term health isn't worth our investment today."

Research and development costs for new drugs can run into the billions of dollars, depending on the condition being addressed, data, and modeling assumptions. There is no doubt that established and even new pharmaceutical companies that make it to market with new and expensive drugs generate more than tidy profits.

A recent example is for a drug newly approved by the FDA for the treatment of early-stage and metastatic breast cancer. The cost of the drug is approximately $8,000 as of this writing for a "21 Tablet Therapy Pack Box." Many insurers have not yet covered the drug or otherwise included it in their prescription drug formulary. But the news media assures us that, "don't worry," the insurers soon will cover the cost of this encouraging treatment. The prediction is more than likely, but with reluctant acceptance by the health insurers, having had inadequate time and warning to work financial models and to increase premiums to cover the costs.

Insurers hate new pharmaceutical wonder drugs!

Whisper Number 5 – "Slow and cheap are better than fast and good."

True story!

A generally healthy man in his early sixties goes for months at a time with no symptoms whatsoever, walks regularly, travels, drives, even engages in the occasional rigorous bicycle ride — all with seemingly little or mostly no pain whatsoever. But now and then, even the slightest movement results in immediate pain, sometimes numbness in the legs, tingling, and weakness. Heck, he was just turning and reaching for his morning coffee, and here we are again!

After a few years of intermittent episodes, the gentleman finally schedules an appointment with his primary care physician to discuss his inconsistent but recurring lower back pain — sciatica. Over-the-counter pain and anti-inflammatory medications are prescribed along with ice packs and rest. The physician suggests that if things don't get better in time, it may make sense to see a specialist, an orthopedic surgeon.

Back surgery? No, thank you!

A similar pattern of alternating periods from pain-free to immobilization continues, despite the addition of rest, ibuprofen, ice packs, and cautious return to regular movement. Enough is enough. Although the patient is passionately opposed to surgery to resolve his pain, he agrees to an imaging study to better determine the cause of the issue.

MRI (Magnetic Resonance Imaging), non-invasive and yielding detailed images, is tolerable and acceptable to the patient. The MRI is scheduled at a familiar and highly reputed hospital very near the patient's home. Scheduled for more than a month out, the next several weeks have the patient both anxious about the possible diagnosis and eager to figure out the culprit.

Just a few weeks prior to the scheduled appointment, the patient receives an unexpected call from the insurance company covering the patient via an employer-provided plan:

> "Hello. This is Care Manager from Blues Plan. We see that you have an MRI scheduled in eleven days, on March 19.", the caller stated.

> "Yes, I do. Is there a problem?", the patient mildly agitated and nervously replied.

"No, there isn't a problem. We are just calling to confirm that your appointment is scheduled at Nearby Really Nice hospital. Right?"

"Yes, that's right."

"The hospital where you have the MRI scheduled is top rate, but they charge well over $1,400 for the MRI. A facility in another part of town will do the test for only $454. Can we work to get you rescheduled for the test at that other facility? If so, we can pre-authorize the claim for the test immediately."

"That facility is probably 40-50 minutes away in heavy traffic, and I'm not at all familiar with that outfit. I'd rather stick with the appointment I already have scheduled. The hospital is nearby, I've been there before, and I've been happy with the care I received there."

"Yes, we understand. But the hospital charges are quite high, so we wanted to provide an alternative."

"Don't you negotiate rates with the various healthcare providers in your network? Doesn't it seem odd to you that one provider charges so much more than another for the same service? It sounds to me like YOU have an issue, not me!"

"Yes, we do negotiate rates with ALL the providers in our network. But we were not able to negotiate better rates with this prestigious hospital. That's why we are recommending that you reschedule your test with an alternate provider."

"No matter what, I have insurance coverage though, don't I?"

"Of course you are covered. However, are you aware that you have a high-deductible plan? And because you haven't yet met your deductible this year, you will need to pay for this test yourself out of pocket to meet the deductible. Having the test done at the facility I suggested will save you roughly a thousand dollars."

"Yes, I know I have a high-deductible plan, that's all that was offered by my employer. However, because I have regular check-ups and follow-up visits, and with healthcare costs the way they are, I hit my deductible every damned year. So, even though I would be out-of-pocket for this test, it won't matter to me by the time the year is up because I will have had to pay out the full amount of my high deductible anyway. So, I will stick with the MRI appointment I already have scheduled."

"But....uh....never mind....OK, thank you."

A couple of things are going on here with this insurance company that highlight their "slow and cheap" bias. Most obviously, the insurer knows well that the patient is likely to hit his deductible at some point during the year, at which point the insurer will be on the hook for claims payments that exceed the achieved high deductible. Mitigating the cost for claims payments that the insurer will need to bear later in the year is one priority. In contrast, the insured member's portion of the claims payments for the year is fixed at the deductible amount plus whatever co-pay is called for under the plan. The higher overall annual healthcare claims costs for an individual are ultimately the insurance company's burden. And, to make matters even worse for the insurance company, the earlier the insured member meets or has made payments against that high deductible, the sooner the insurance company will make payments for medical claims exceeding the deductible amount. That is, the insurer's cash is going out the door earlier in the year than the insurance company cares to spend — cash that could otherwise be retained and invested to generate bottom-line profits to the insurance company (see Whisper Number 2).

The other issue at hand here, an only slightly less obvious strategy being employed, is to put some pressure on Nearby Really Nice Hospital to reduce the charges for the tests or procedures that can otherwise be obtained for significantly lower cost at nearby facilities. That age-old threat to move precious volumes for tests and procedures to other facilities may or may not be perceived as a real danger. With patient access to any variety of healthcare services increasingly difficult, Nearby Really Nice Hospital may not care that a few tests or procedures are referred elsewhere. Their operating rooms, ambulatory surgery centers, imaging departments, and laboratories are fully booked regardless. Nevertheless, providers' historical thinking and mantra is that volumes rule the day. Even a small but measurable decline in the volumes — coupled with the perception that tests and procedures are being referred elsewhere due to the facility's high-cost structure — might yield a willingness to negotiate, although likely offset by the increased expense of some other test or procedure where the facility is in high demand or even in a monopoly position to dictate yet higher prices. Insurance companies are rarely (if ever) going to be bothered by slower and cheaper — or, for that matter, denied or avoided altogether.

Whisper Number 6 – "Regulators are a bit of a nuisance, but they don't get in our way."

While many insurance companies operate across the U.S. or even internationally, insurance regulation varies from state to state in the U.S., with each state operating under its own set of statutes and rules. It's a bit of a nuisance for a multi-state insurer, needing to understand the regulatory landscape and rules and regulations that vary between the regions in which they operate. Understanding politics is also a bother, with the top Insurance Commissioner elected in only eleven (11) of the nation's states and appointed in the other 39 states. What about the National Association of Insurance Commissioners (NAIC)? Aren't they really in charge? Well, no. They're there to provide support and analysis to the state regulators, but with limited oversight and power.

Insurer solvency is high on the list of priorities for the state insurance departments. For long and well-established health insurance companies, solvency is rarely, if ever, an issue. On the contrary, some regulators often get testy at health insurers' over-capitalization, sometimes pressuring insurers to lower their premiums to mitigate the decades of cumulative surplus. Now, that's a serious annoyance!

Ultimately, health insurers know that they must "be nice" to the regulators but aren't afraid to engage in the battles that are most likely to benefit their bottom line, fighting against the rate increase denial, for example. The health insurers' competitive advantage lies in the knowledge that the state regulators have their hands full. Insurance commissioners' offices are often understaffed and overwhelmed with issues that span all insurance types, not just health care coverage. Health insurance is on their list, but so is life insurance, long-term disability and most visible, property and casualty, especially time and resource consumption in recent years due to the claims associated with climate change and natural catastrophes. This discordant focus for the regulators is understandably overwhelming as they address and respond to countless customer complaints that range from nuisance to very serious, keeping up with changes in the laws, all in an organizational environment that is likely to change with the next election or appointment of any state's top regulatory official. In the end, insurers play nicely and tolerate insurance regulators, but mostly in the back of their collective insurer minds.

Whisper Number 7 – "We have no idea which doctors are better than others, let alone which you should avoid"

And they don't really care. With decades of claims data and access to all sorts of information required as part of experienced credentialing processes, it's reasonable to believe that health insurers have at least a broad sense of which doctors are the best and which to avoid. I (Bela) had the opportunity to ask that question of a top executive of a sky-colored (Blues plan) West Coast health insurer. The executive answered honestly that their information about better or less desirable physicians relied almost exclusively on word of mouth. Subjective Yelp reviews appear to be the most accessible resource to consumers. In fairness, obtaining and assessing objective quality data is still in the early stages. Data is being increasingly collected for statistics ranging from patient satisfaction to appropriate versus unnecessary testing and screenings. Appropriateness of procedures and patient outcomes are data that are materially more challenging to collect. Gaming statistics in this burgeoning area of data collection is also tricky, as the physicians and other healthcare providers have no real incentive to share unfavorable information. Ultimately, and gloomily, while a robust ranking of physician healthcare providers may be beneficial to consumers, resources necessary to enhance health insurers' bottom line in this area are better spent elsewhere.

Whisper Number 8 – "End-of-life is expensive, so we hope you wrap it up quickly."

Not so much a whisper, but an obvious annoyance for insurers when considering the cost of dying in the U.S. As much as 25% of all Medicare expenses are estimated to result from expenses at end of life. With many large insurers participating and taking risks with Medicare beneficiaries through Medicare Advantage, Accountable Care Organizations, supplemental benefit, and even federal/state-sponsored innovation programs, the cost to insurers is a real bother. The matter is further complicated by individual, and family wishes to extend life as well as an overwhelming willingness for the medical community to do so. We hear of patients dying from complications related to chronic kidney disease less than 24 hours after having received dialysis; radiation treatments for patients with various and even multiple cancer diagnoses within weeks or even days prior to passing; and my (Bela) experience of an elderly family member submitting to a complicated craniotomy surgery (cutting into the skull for brain surgery) to address an intracranial hemorrhage just a very few months prior to his death in a hospice facility. The personal, spiritual, community, cultural, and medical community considerations are extensive and complex. We all know how it's ultimately going to end. Insurers would prefer to simply mitigate or better yet entirely avoid the expense. Please die quickly.

Chapter Seven: All Things Being Equal: They Aren't

With all our system has to offer, it can emphatically be said that everyone does not experience the same healthcare system. The Centers for Medicare & Medicaid Services (CMS) define Health Equity ***as the attainment of the highest level of health for all people, where everyone has a fair and just opportunity to attain their optimal health regardless of race, ethnicity, disability, sexual orientation, gender identity, socioeconomic status, geography, preferred language, or other factors that affect access to care and health outcomes.*** The strategic plan developed to make needed improvements, put forward during the Biden/Harris administration, is already being ignored, dropped, and thwarted under the newest administration.

In late 2024, Indigenous Pact, PBC leadership met in Montgomery, Alabama for their leadership retreat. The retreat included a visit to the Equal Justice Initiative's legacy sites, which memorialize the extensive and brutal history of slavery in the United States. If you have never visited these sites in Montgomery, I (Jim) highly recommend it. The two and a half days were impactful personally and professionally, and as a baby boomer white male, I can assure you it was a humbling experience. As a team, we met throughout the retreat to reflect on what we had seen and learned, and we also discussed materials assigned for advanced preparation. Conversations were often emotional; we all had a shared belief that such hate and terrorism can never be allowed to happen again, nor should it be forgotten. Kurt and Amee, a husband-and-wife team, founded Indigenous Pact to address healthcare inequities among Native Americans and Alaskan Natives within a single generation. Understanding injustices and inequities can't just be words on paper — they must translate into actions. The retreat was a way for Kurt and Amee to help the team get to know each other better and in a different way; it also grounded our work through understanding and being compelled to act.

There is no doubt a lot written and said about health equity. Yet, measuring the effectiveness of efforts to improve it can be akin to playing a game of Whack-a-Mole. Not only are there health disparities across those categories set forth by CMS, but a well-connected healthcare insider is much more likely to get their loved ones or a friend access to services than less connected individuals—i.e., "privilege." Recently, I (Jim) had a family member battling a neurological condition, desiring but struggling to get an expert second opinion. I contacted someone I knew at a highly regarded healthcare organization and was able to help navigate the next steps. This re-raised the question in my mind: what do other people do when faced with this maze of specialty types, institutions, and in-network limitations? It can be a struggle for me, and I am an insider.

A November 17, 2023, article published at the University of Southern California identifies six types of health disparities and offers some ideas on how to address them — none of them easy in our current system. There are some areas improving across the board, while there are some that are not. We see disparities in mortality rates between the educated and the uneducated, between racial lines, across various states, and even across different counties within states — and certainly between rural and urban populations. We see disparities in life expectancy for Black and Latino people. As for who carries the greatest burden of any particular disease, there are many examples, such as the fact that American Indians/Alaska Natives have the highest rates of diagnosed diabetes. There are many disparities when it comes to access to mental health treatment. There are gender disparities, race and socio-economic disparities. Another area where disparities exist is between the insured and underinsured. There are plenty of causes that result in racial and geographic disparities, not the least of which is the decision not to expand the Medicaid programs in certain states. Finally, there are all sorts of barriers for access to healthcare that create disparities between rural and urban, race, income, and educated and uneducated. In some cases, services simply don't exist in proximity. Even when insured, healthcare can be expensive, and some simply have to avoid getting care or doing the things they need to prevent their own illness (such as healthy foods).

In perhaps one of the most striking examples, Native Americans are more likely to have diabetes, heart disease, TB, and cancer at higher rates than other Americans. What follows is a set of interviews between co-author Bela Biro and Native American leadership at Indigenous Pact, PBC (IP):

> **BB:** What personal experiences or family histories inspired you to dedicate your career to addressing healthcare inequities among Native American and Alaskan Native communities?
>
> **IP:** This is a big question, and something I think about a lot in my daily work. I grew up on the Flathead Indian Reservation, which is in northwest Montana. It belongs to the Confederated Salish and Kootenai Tribes, of which I am a descendant. My mother's side of the family is Salish and Crow, which is a tribe residing in southeastern Montana. My ancestral tribes are on opposite sides of the entire state—and it's a very big state—and I've spent time equally on both reservations.
>
> I spent 27 years of my life on the reservation. I think in terms of just general upbringing and the status of how American Indians operate on rural reservations, family is at the core. I grew up with a single mother. She was really all I had. My grandparents were instrumental in my upbringing, picking up a lot of the slack and showing me a lot about what it means to grow up Native.
>
> I find my role in healthcare interesting because my grandmother was one of the first American Indians to truly

consider how urban Indians are impacted by a lack of healthcare. Back in her day, they only had the Indian Health Service or personal insurance if you wanted to access healthcare. In her life, she observed the healthcare needs of many Native people. With that recognition, she established one of the first urban Indian health organizations in Montana. She was deeply passionate about providing healthcare to American Indians and Alaska Natives, regardless of their location. It's truly remarkable to see how my academic and professional path has increasingly gravitated toward this area of healthcare.

Both sides of my family were dedicated to helping Indigenous peoples. My grandfather was one of the first American Indian lawyers in the country. He attended law school to assist the Crow Tribe with any needs they might have. I grew up in a highly activist household, something I am incredibly grateful for. It made me acutely aware of the various forms of discrimination our people have faced. My mother shared stories of discrimination she experienced as a child. My grandparents were often turned away from restaurants and denied service in certain establishments. They met at Montana State University and were among the first Native people to receive a higher education. This wasn't that long ago.

When considering healthcare equity, you must also look at the various social determinants of health and upward mobility. American Indians haven't had the opportunity to create these for themselves due to our long history of colonization, assimilation, forced removal from our traditional territories, and the enduring impact of historical trauma. Witnessing my grandparents' generation striving for upward mobility with many obstacles is something I didn't fully grasp as a child. Now, with a deeper understanding of how individuals navigate social mobility, I realize that I'm only just two generations removed from their struggles and accomplishments.

One of the interesting things I discovered upon entering the "real world" was that, growing up and utilizing our tribal healthcare system, everything I needed was in a single building. I could simply walk into my tribal health clinic and access various services: behavioral health, eye exams, dental care, pharmacy, and primary care. All of these services were housed under one roof in my hometown. However, scheduling appointments for each of these services was incredibly challenging. It felt like a "use it or lose it" system. Appointments were often booked three months in advance, and if you missed one, you might have to wait an entire year for another. I believe the way time functions within this system—the long wait times and difficulty in scheduling—significantly hinders people's ability to engage in preventative care. For example, if I had an abscessed tooth, I had two options: I could get it treated at the tribal clinic at no cost to me, or I could go to an emergency dental clinic and pay out of pocket. Another option is waiting for a dental referral to an acute care dentist, but that often adds more time and steps. Considering that many people in our community live in poverty, struggle to make ends meet, or prioritize their families' needs over their own healthcare, they are more likely to choose the option that avoids immediate financial expense. Unfortunately, delaying treatment for a dental abscess can have serious consequences, potentially impacting other parts of the body.

Delaying the care is easier, including on your wallet. But the return is that your health is negatively impacted later. It's a push and pull where you don't want to spend money, but because of not spending money, you prolong whatever chronic illness you have or whatever is going on with your body. You are probably decreasing your own longevity.

BB: Are the long wait times and difficulty scheduling simply a function of supply and demand—that is, the supply of providers and the demands of the community?

IP: Yes. One of the biggest issues that we see in tribal clinics, whether it is a tribally operated one or an Indian Health Service clinic in a rural area or even a city, is just that there is such high turnover of providers. It's hard to establish a good relationship with your provider so that you feel comfortable in the healthcare setting enough to tell them about your body. The turnover also contributes to the difficulty of getting on a regular cadence of seeing your provider on an annual or biannual basis, and this is pretty much the same in all those different areas. It's particularly hard to find dentists. We have a lot of dental assistants, and there are some great tribal colleges and local colleges that are really pushing American Indians and Alaska Natives to get involved in nursing. So, we have a lot of those, which is great. But we don't have a lot of actual providers. For example, for five days a week, you have two dentists that are operating from 9 to 5, working all day, seeing people from all walks of life. And not only is that taxing for the provider, but also if that provider is away due to illness or other reasons, fewer patients will be seen.

With that limited supply of providers, there's more and more buildup of chronic issues in our community. The lack of providers is due not only to high turnover but also because many providers just don't want to live in the areas that we live in. The rural areas of Montana are cold most of the time, and there is a lack of housing on the reservations and in rural areas, making it almost impossible to own anything or even to rent. Or living in that environment is just not what a provider from an urban upbringing and lifestyle may want. So, providers don't live in the areas where they work, and they must commute. That makes it difficult. When considering all these social determinants of health, and the currently emerging concept of Indigenous determinants of health, it becomes clear that housing is fundamental to healthcare. Secure housing provides not only physical safety and shelter but also contributes to overall well-being—not just for these providers, but for our own people. In rural areas, increased housing availability can significantly improve healthcare outcomes by attracting and retaining healthcare providers, allowing them to establish a long-term presence in the community, and providing safety and shelter for many unhoused Native people.

BB: Do you believe it's feasible to see a substantial decrease in U.S. healthcare disparities in the near future?

IP: I think it's possible. It doesn't mean it's easy, but I do think it's possible. There are so many issues to fix, and if you're thinking about healthcare equity as a whole, it can be really daunting to figure out where to start. Just thinking about how the healthcare system operates within the larger structures of what makes people have poor health outcomes, there's a lot of work to be done.

Sometimes we want a quick fix because that's what we're used to, and it's honestly just going to take generations of people who are sick of the systems and the infrastructures that keep disenfranchised communities down. And the ability of individuals to have the privilege and the upward mobility to even be able to participate in and change those systems. Because I think sometimes, we still have a large population of our people who are just trying to survive. And in that state of survival, nobody has time to think about the infrastructures and systems that are keeping us down. Organizations including Indigenous Pact and scholars and others are working to change these systems. Generation after generation, we're slowly going to be able to solve some of the issues.

I look to my mother and stepfather and think about all the hardships they endured in their childhood, particularly the challenges they faced as American Indians in this world. They worked incredibly hard on their own personal growth and education, overcoming obstacles that I thankfully don't have to face to the same degree.

BB: Can you discuss the challenges of promoting dietary guidelines like the Mediterranean diet in Native American and Alaskan Native communities, where traditional foodways and access to culturally appropriate foods play a vital role in health and well-being?

IP: Well, we don't live in the Mediterranean! What does that mean to Indigenous people? They want to eat what they're accustomed to eating.

The general paradigm in America is to push this Western agenda and this Western way of living, no matter what group you come from or what community you belong to. And that's why we have this food pyramid that stresses Western carbohydrates, Western fruits and vegetables, and dairy. Indigenous people are lactose intolerant and have been since time immemorial because we didn't have cows. There's no record of any sort of milking of animals in our communities, so we're not biologically equipped to digest it. So, when people say, "Oh, you need more calcium, you should just drink milk," it's like, "Okay, well, my body's not equipped for that. I'll get sick."

Those lines definitely blur as well. I think it took me going to the East Coast—I got my undergraduate degree at Yale University—and it took me leaving the reservation and going to this Ivy League institution and studying food systems to realize, "Oh wow, I live in a food desert. The community I grew up in has limited access to healthy and nutritious foods." And I can see chronic illnesses because of that.

It's crazy to go to other countries and just see how they're functioning. But just looking at how those countries function in their systems, like having public transportation more readily available. Everybody in Amsterdam is on their bike or walking. People have more healthy habits that are built into the fabric of their society. And we just don't have that in the U.S.

As I'm pursuing my Ph.D. at Montana State University in Indigenous and Rural Health, we talk a lot about these things. One of the things that I believe is that if we made a slow return to our traditional ways of living, we would just be healthier people. But because we've been so far removed from that—and violently removed from that—we operate within this Western system that we were just not meant to be in. We don't walk. We don't get outside. We sit most of the time. We're consuming Western foods that were forcibly pushed onto us. And food is an addiction. I mean, there's a reason why they use rats to study sugar and stuff like that.

If we just, generation by generation, get back to what our ancestors did, we would just be healthier as people. And honestly, I also think that a lot of the Indigenous modalities of health and wellness—if the rest of America participated in some of that—I think we would also be healthier as a nation. It's my firm belief that Indigenous people were among the healthiest people on the planet prior to colonization because we were out engaging with the land, we were engaging with our communities, with our families. We had a sense of self and identity. We participated in a very hyper-local, hyper-seasonal food system, and we had access to clean air and clean water. And those largely don't quite exist in the systems that we function within now.

BB: Can you describe Indigenous Pact's mission and vision? What specific strategies is the organization employing to address healthcare inequities within Indigenous communities?

IP: I've been with Indigenous Pact for five years. It was one of my first and only "big girl" jobs, which was incredibly lucky for me because I was a master's student when I joined. I didn't really know what I wanted to be when I grew up. I had been studying food systems, exploring how Indigenous food systems have drastically changed over time and how this has significantly impacted our overall health. I was also specifically looking into my Salish community and how the historical transition to this Westernized lifestyle has contributed to the high prevalence of chronic illnesses within our population.

Then, a great guy named Kurt Brenkus and I got connected after a colleague of his met me at a graduate networking event. (CEO of Indigenous Pact, a company that focuses on health and healthcare delivery for American Indians and Alaska Natives). He asked me about my studies, and after I explained my research, he invited me to do some contracting work with Indigenous Pact, focusing on food systems and traditional foods.

As time went on, the organization continued to involve me in their consulting work. I've been involved in a diverse range of projects across various areas, and I've learned a tremendous amount about healthcare, health equity, and how we can effectively reform the systems that currently impact American Indian and Alaska Native people.

Essentially, Indigenous Pact is a company dedicated to creating health equity for American Indians and Alaska Natives. We achieve this through a couple of key strategies:

Consulting: This is the area where I initially began. We offer a wide range of consulting services to tribal entities, including:

- Feasibility studies
- Reviews of billing and coding within their clinic systems

- "Food as Medicine" program development
- Support for Veterans Health and Youth Wellness centers, among many others.

Clinic Development and Management: We build, operate, and manage clinics, or co-manage them with tribal entities. A significant focus has been on establishing substance use disorder (SUD) treatment programs, specifically Outpatient Treatment Programs (OTPs). These clinics have proven to be highly effective within the communities we serve.

While addressing health inequities is paramount, it's also important to acknowledge economic realities. We understand the importance of financial sustainability for tribal communities. One key aspect of our clinic-based approach is that these clinics often serve both Native and non-Native patients. By serving a broader patient population, these clinics receive higher reimbursement rates. This increased revenue can then be reinvested back into the community by the tribe itself. This could include:

- Building a gym or wellness center
- Investing in walking paths
- Providing food for elders or youth
- Supporting other vital community programs.

Essentially, these generated funds allow the tribe to exercise its sovereignty and invest in initiatives that best suit their community's needs.

Exploring Innovative Models of Care: We are constantly exploring new and innovative models of care within our clinic operations. One of my most impactful projects has been the development of a dialysis clinic on the Northern Cheyenne Reservation in Montana.

Many Northern Cheyenne tribal members must travel two hours to Billings, the nearest city, to receive dialysis treatment. This arduous journey, coupled with the burden of their chronic illness, often leads to significant challenges in adhering to their treatment plans. Many patients become discouraged and choose to discontinue their dialysis treatments altogether. By establishing a dialysis clinic on the reservation, we aim to improve access to care, reduce the significant burden of travel, and ultimately improve the quality of life for these individuals. True healthcare equity is not about forcing individuals to conform to existing systems, but rather about adapting and reforming those systems to meet the unique needs of the communities we serve.

BB: How do you ensure that Indigenous communities are actively involved in decision-making and program development?

IP: We work directly with tribes, recognizing their sovereignty. Tribes have a government-to-government relationship with the federal government. In the example of the dialysis clinic, the tribe in Montana came to us and explained that they wanted to provide dialysis on the reservation so our people can start living their lives again. The need for accessible dialysis services is particularly critical in Montana, a vast state with limited healthcare resources where Indigenous populations experience a higher prevalence of end-stage renal disease, often requiring long-distance travel for treatment. Driving for hours to receive dialysis treatment is not only inconvenient but also emotionally and physically taxing. These long journeys can significantly impact a patient's overall health and well-being. We responded by explaining that we would help to provide all of the tools to successfully implement this project. We understand that tribal healthcare systems may not have extensive experience with specialized services like dialysis, which are often dominated by a few large corporations. Ultimately, our goal is to empower tribes to independently operate their own healthcare services, tailored to the specific needs and cultural values of their communities.

Leveraging our expertise in healthcare, we brought together a team of clinicians, doctors, and management professionals to guide the tribe through the process. We helped them understand how to:

- Establish and maintain a sustainable dialysis clinic.
- Navigate the complexities of billing and coding within the healthcare system.
- Ensure long-term financial viability for the clinic.

This experience underscored the critical importance of this project. It demonstrated the profound impact that accessible healthcare can have on the well-being of Indigenous communities and serves as a model for other tribes to follow. During the groundbreaking ceremony for the new dialysis clinic on the Northern Cheyenne Reservation, a poignant reminder of the impact of this project emerged. Chairs were lined up to represent each community member who had tragically succumbed to end-stage renal disease. In a small community, the loss of 50 individuals to this illness is a significant and deeply felt tragedy.

By empowering tribes to take control of their own healthcare destinies, we can work together to improve the health and well-being of Indigenous communities across the nation—and simply provide the opportunity for individuals to be back with their families and spending more time just being people.

The following chart compares mortality rates (deaths per 100,000 population) between American Indians/Alaska Natives (AI/AN) and the overall U.S. population for various causes of death. The "Ratio: AI/AN to US All Races" column reveals how many times higher the mortality rate is for AI/AN individuals compared to the national average. For example, with a ratio of 6.6, AI/AN are 6.6 times more likely to die from alcohol-related causes and have a 2.5 times higher risk of accidental death than the general U.S. population.

IHS Mortality Disparity Rates (AI/AN to US All Races)

Causes	AI/AN Rate (deaths per 100,000)	U.S All Races Rate	Ratio: AI/AN to US All Races
Alcohol-induced	50.0	38.0	6.6
Chronic liver disease and cirrhosis	42.9	9.4	4.6
Diabetes mellitus (diabetes)	66.0	20.8	3.2
Accidents (unintentional injuries)*	93.7	38.0	2.5
Assault (homicide)	11.4	5.4	2.1
Influenza and pneumonia	26.6	15.1	1.8
Intentional self-harm (suicide)	20.4	12.1	1.7
Drug-induced	23.4	15.3	1.5
Nephritis, nephrotic syndrome (kidney disease)	22.4	15.3	1.5

Health disparities among Native Americans, just as with many other segments of our population, can be attributed to a "one-size-fits-all" system that is designed to reflect and serve only a fragment of our diverse culture. Just as some in our country have embraced Eastern medicine techniques, we have much to learn from our collective diversity when it comes to other cultures' traditional forms of medicine and what constitutes a healthy lifestyle. Our current system of education, prevention, and treatment makes little use of this valuable asset. We thank the team at Indigenous Pact for shedding more light on the opportunities to build stronger communities through awareness.

Chapter Eight: A System empowered to say "No"

One of the most aggravating aspects of the U.S. healthcare system is how adept it has become at creating barriers to delivering care and preventative services. There is a systemically created culture that suffocates innovation and unwittingly empowers everyone involved in paying for or delivering services to say no.

Examples are almost limitless, and some seem more absurd than others. Most are rooted in regulatory complexity and overreach, anti-competitive behaviors, the economic realities of the system, and even in a lack of compassion and empathy by provider organizations.

The most obvious and probably most often experienced by average consumers is an insurance company's proclivity to deny claims. Of course, why not? This goes to the heart of profitability in the industry. Populations are assessed by actuaries (experts in math and statistics evaluating risk and uncertainty), and insurance companies assume the risk that paying for the care delivered to a population of people (their costs) will be less than the premiums paid to them by individuals and employers to purchase coverage (their revenue). It is a bet that the house must — and always will — win.

A group purchasing and consulting organization, Premier, found that hospitals and health systems spent an estimated $19.7 billion in 2022 trying to overturn denied claims. Denied claims tended to be more prevalent for higher-cost treatments, with the average denial attributed to charges of $14,000 or more. Almost 15% of all claims submitted to private insurance are initially denied, including many that were preapproved during the prior authorization process, with insurance companies heading off services that are presumably not medically necessary to some standard or another — or, as is often the case, simply not a benefit covered under the individual's healthcare insurance policy. Overall, 15.7% of Medicare Advantage and 13.9% of commercial claims were initially denied. More than half of the claims denied (54.3%) by payers were overturned, but not until providers went through multiple rounds of costly refiling. So, our system —

designed to say "no" — adds costs to those delivering and receiving care by creating a robust layer of administrative resistance.

This decree is especially puzzling, particularly in what many claim is a free market designed for competition and top performance. How many consumers are aware that hospitals are often constrained to a limited number of licensed beds? At least thirty-five states and the District of Columbia have systems in place to limit major equipment, build new facilities, or expand their services. Hospitals must secure a Certificate of Need (CON) to expand the number of beds they have, all in the name of ensuring costly redundant services are not wasted. These are not just small hoops to jump through, they are substantive hurdles companies must surpass if they want to grow their service footprint. This requirement seems extremely odd in an industry that many believe should succumb to a free capitalist market mentality. Isn't it true that when supply exceeds demand, prices fall? This is the sort of thing supporting the assertion that healthcare is not a rational market.

This one applies to many professions across the healthcare spectrum, and it has become so normalized that no one really questions it anymore. Imagine spending many years going through undergraduate school, then postgraduate studies, and working your way through internships and residency programs to become a medical doctor. You excelled in all your training from fully accredited programs and are excited to begin your career. You imagine a career that may include in-person and virtual services, and you also live near a bordering state. You can't just apply for a license to practice medicine once — you have to get a license from each state where you may be providing services. Each state licensing board has its own criteria. Reviewing the American Medical Association's website to learn how to navigate this mess provides clarity regarding what a bureaucratic maze physicians must endure. Do we really want a national healthcare system that is partially regulated by the state and partially regulated by the federal government? Is there any reason to think that doctors in one state should be of any lower or higher quality than another? Licensures of all kinds, whether for a particular profession or to be allowed to deliver a particular service, are especially onerous and create market barriers that limit supply — and therefore drive higher prices.

With the Dobbs decision overturning Roe v. Wade, we have seen how the system can be set up to simply say NO to people in times of great peril. By now, we have all heard many of the horrific stories of women left to bleed out in their cars because caregivers were not allowed to intervene in a failing pregnancy until the mother's life was threatened. Our politization of healthcare as a set of moral choices rather than decisions to be made by individuals, families, and healthcare providers adds one more layer of complexity.

There are many other ways in which our system says "no" to the sort of care that our communities need. There are often barriers to access such as cost, geographic proximity, and supply. These barriers are also due to something those in the industry refer to as "payer mix."

What is payer mix? Payer mix represents the proportion of the organization's patient community covered by each major payer. If a hospital or group medical practice has a high commercial payer mix, it means that a high percentage of its patients are commercially insured rather than covered by Medicare or the state's Medicaid plan(s). Reimbursement is typically — but not always — more favorable than government-sponsored plans. So, to have a "healthy" payer mix means that you are more likely to have a healthier bottom line. Because of the wide range of reimbursement to providers for identical services from different payers, it behooves them to closely monitor and manage their payer mix.

While many nonprofit and for-profit provider organizations like to tout their service to the underserved, they also like to remind their caregivers: "No money, no mission." This doesn't mean someone stands at the door and checks to see what insurance you have so they can accept only patients representing their desired payer mix. But managing the payer mix affects where they place their services (neighborhoods), who their marketing campaigns are intended to target, and not target. If provider organizations could simply deny care to all Medicaid patients, they say, life would be grand!

These more macro examples are largely unknown background to consumers, but the foreground often sounds something like this:

> *"We don't have anything available on weekends"*
>
> *"You'll have to schedule a separate visit for that"*
>
> *"Please be here fifteen minutes early. If you are not on time, we will have to reschedule your appointment"*
>
> *"We are not accepting new patients"*
>
> *"We can't schedule the procedure until you get prior approval from your insurance carrier"*
>
> *"I'm sorry, we don't accept your insurance"*

The U.S. healthcare system is regulated in many dysfunctional areas and at each layer of its irrational maze of stakeholders. Provider organizations regulate access to care, local and state governments regulate licensures of professionals and medical services, both federal and state governments regulate what is required of insurance companies, and both politics and religion influence how all these disparate participants function, or most often how they do not. Working towards a solution to address patients and community through service and prevention will serve our population versus the current culture and overwhelming bias to say *NO*.

Chapter Nine: It's Not All Their Fault

Ideally, we'd all be healthy and well, never needing to go to the doctor or hospital, aside from the occasional need for medications to improve or maintain our health. The reality, however, is that it really doesn't matter how many salads we consume or how much we exercise. MDs will remind us that our bodies are, in fact, machines and machines break down over time. Genetics, environmental and societal factors, plagues, pandemics, fights, wars, accidents, aging... something's going to get us. That is, we all die (great title for a book, huh?). And in the meantime, we, as Homo sapiens, an intelligent species (supposedly), remain vulnerable. Nevertheless, we tend to search for easy and quick solutions to health and longevity.

We became fascinated with the Blue Zones — those geographic regions of the world where people live longer and with lower rates of chronic diseases than the average population. For many years, we were told that a glass of red wine per day was the answer, like the Sardinians, particularly in certain regions, with their higher-than-average life expectancy. Recent studies suggest that robust reds were less significant than the genetic predisposition of various family lines within the Sardinian population. Perhaps the next generation would be well served by childbearing with native Sardinians — a difficult strategy, at best.

Blue Zones and genetics notwithstanding — and left with countless health issues — can we fully blame doctors and a broken healthcare system when much of our food supply is poisonous, nutritious food is unavailable or unaffordable, many individuals are missing the dietary knowledge or culinary skills to prepare healthy meals, exercise is inadequate, the environment increasingly toxic, social norms encourage unhealthy habits, and even genetics vary widely? Things like where we live, our economic status, the quality of our education, access to safe and affordable housing, the level of stress we experience, and our environment significantly influence our health and well-being.

The idea that social factors significantly impact health has been recognized for centuries, including early links between poverty and disease outbreaks. Post-World War II public health movements emphasized the importance of addressing social issues like housing, sanitation, and access to clean water to improve overall population health. More recently, the term Social Determinants of Health (SDOH) has been increasingly recognized and emphasized — although yet only minimally addressed in the U.S.

Indeed, assessing an individual's SDOH is challenging and complex. There is no standardized set of questions or tools. Many SDOH, like stress levels or social support, are subjective and difficult to accurately quantify. Nevertheless, physicians are increasingly asked to document patients' SDOH in their clinical setting's Electronic Medical Record (EMR). Busy clinicians mostly view these documentation requirements as yet another added burden to their already overloaded schedules. Patients are often reluctant to provide the information expressing concern about privacy violations despite policies and assurances that their information is safe and protected. So, this step is often skipped or glossed over by the clinician.

Sadly, beyond the blame that is often justifiably directed toward our fundamentally flawed and broken healthcare system, our issues are much greater and more fundamental. That is, it can be said that the health of our society is systemic — the result of a societal structure that has placed higher value on consumerism, entertainment, military spending, and fun than on education, housing, and healthy lifestyles with accompanying high-quality healthcare for the population.

The reality is frustrating as hell for clinicians who accept the lion's share of the criticism for our country's poor population health. Many will explain that they are willing to accept some of the responsibility for the nation's poor health but argue that only about 10% (or so) is attributable to the medical profession. A primary care physician summed it up well, explaining, "Why should I be blamed when my morbidly obese patient with heart issues leaves my office after having been counseled, only to stop at a fast-food restaurant to consume a 30% fat hamburger that he (or she) will dip in mayonnaise, with a side of French fries plunged in sugary ketchup or ranch dressing?"

On the other hand — and fortunately — the percentage of adults smoking cigarettes has significantly decreased over time, according to the Centers for Disease Control and Prevention (CDC). This significant improvement has mitigated many other damaging factors contributing to the nation's health decline. And while invoking the CDC's reporting on smoking, consider that, as of this writing, the recently confirmed Secretary of the Department of Health and Human Services — newly overseeing the CDC — Robert F. Kennedy Jr., has remarked that the federal agency's vaccine division is a "fascist enterprise" and accused it of knowingly harming children. He also compared what he saw as a widespread conspiracy to hide harms from the childhood vaccination program to the cover-up of child sexual abuse in the Catholic Church. This is where those who safeguard our population from the threats of disease may now be getting their marching orders — at least in the near term.

Let's look at morbid obesity, a very visible and highly significant factor in health, often contributing to heart disease, type 2 diabetes, sleep apnea, certain cancers, and shortened life expectancy. The U.S. leads all developed countries in rates of morbid obesity, with some states reporting obesity rates over 70%. What can clinicians do about it? Strong recommendations, diet programs, expensive surgeries including gastric bypass, gastric banding, and even saline-filled balloons inserted into the stomach, and increasingly, prescription medications to help with weight loss and appetite suppression. Many — if not most — of these recommendations, treatments, and remedies have been available for decades, and few address the root causes. Once again, the system treats the symptoms and not the cause.

The U.S. adult obesity rate has more than doubled from the early 1990s to over 40% in the early 2020s. The story for children is similar, with the obesity rate nearly doubling over 19% for girls and approaching 22% for boys. It doesn't have to be this way — as evidenced by most European countries, where a widely adopted Mediterranean diet, active lifestyles, and good access to healthcare result in healthier populations and higher life expectancy rates compared to the U.S.

While U.S. healthcare undoubtedly plays a crucial role and must be addressed, we dutifully acknowledge that the root causes surrounding our nation's health crisis are far more complex. Our societal structure — prioritizing consumerism and entertainment over education, healthy lifestyles, and equitable access to healthcare — significantly undermines public health. The prevalence of processed foods, lack of access to nutritious options, and sedentary lifestyles continue to fuel the chronic disease crisis.

Addressing this crisis requires a multi-pronged approach: from public health initiatives to social safety nets that ensure access to affordable housing, quality education, and nutritious food. Most importantly and perhaps most challenging, it will require re-evaluating our cultural and societal priorities to elevate the health and well-being of our population over short-term gains. Individuals, communities, legislators, and healthcare providers will need to sync up to create a healthier and more equitable society.

Chapter Ten: Anecdotes and Observations

Kidding ourselves?

Sometimes it's tempting to ask ourselves, "Is it really as bad as we think? Are we just accustomed to high expectations, and are our demands so great that we don't realize how good we have it?" The data suggests otherwise. Traveling abroad and having conversations punctuates this point. Back to the Italian town of Lucca, Italy.

Despite my (Bela) rusty Italian — my first language, set aside when our family moved to the U.S. during my infancy — I had the opportunity for long conversations, a mix of Italian and English, with Fabrizio, an elderly ceramic artist with a flamboyant flair, in his tiny shop on Via Fillungo, just inside the Porta dei Borghi where it meets Via Michele Rosi. His shop, a treasure trove of handcrafted ceramics in various styles and sizes — all of his own design — was a vibrant reflection of the man himself. Officially, his hours were posted, but Fabrizio, a well-travelled soul fluent in English, was a constant presence, often there even when the shop was supposedly closed. "Just knock," he'd say with a welcoming grin, "if you see me inside."

He'd journeyed across the United States, from New York to Los Angeles, and his passion for cinema — both Italian and American, especially the works of Quentin Tarantino — infused his conversations. He wasn't just selling ceramics; he was sharing stories and a slice of his vibrant, artistic life.

He explained his understanding that, as a tourist traveling in the United States, if an accident, tragedy, or medical emergency occurred, it could mean financial devastation without travel health insurance. I could only agree. He then commented on how different it was in his home country of Italy.

"How so?" I asked.

"Let me tell you a story," he said. *"It will highlight two major differences."*

He explained how, just outside his artisan shop, an elderly American tourist had fallen and injured herself—apparently breaking a bone.

"Number one difference," he explained, *"a few people, and then a larger group, gathered around to see how they could help the woman."* With that many people, some were likely more helpful than others. The difference, he said, was that in the United States—particularly in big cities like New York, where he had previously visited—people would likely not gather. Rather, they would dart off, avoid eye contact, and not even acknowledge the situation. Perhaps there would be a Good Samaritan or two, but more likely, if anything, people would be posting on social media rather than getting involved and assisting—for whatever reason: too busy, fear of lawsuits, embarrassment, or some other conditioning that keeps them from getting involved.

Ultimately, the woman with the broken arm was taken to a nearby hospital. I explained that I didn't know there was a hospital so close to the interior of this ancient walled city. He explained it was not far at all — just beyond the walls. The woman was taken there, X-rayed, and her broken limb was taken care of and set. This was "Difference number two." Grateful for the quick medical treatment, the woman nevertheless feared the financial impact. She was told there would be no charge. *"No,"* she explained, *"I'm not from here. I don't have insurance. This is going to be really expensive."* It was more explicitly explained to her that this was a public hospital, and they take care of sick or injured people. There would be no charge.

Medicare sucks.

Well... not really.

From the insurance company "dark side" to the front lines of patient care, Medicare's policies, payment methods, and communications have rarely escaped disdain and cynicism. As insiders, we scoffed. It was the bureaucratic behemoth, the lumbering giant of reimbursement, the source of endless paperwork and seemingly arbitrary regulations. "Medicare," we'd say, "always a step behind, always complicating things." Yet, while we were busy bemoaning its perceived flaws, Medicare — under the radar — has become a surprising driver of innovation.

It's easy to forget, amidst the daily grind of patient care, that Medicare, despite its size and complexity, has been a consistent, if sometimes unacknowledged, driver of change in the American healthcare landscape. Few outside of Medicare (CMS – Centers for Medicare & Medicaid Services) are aware that there exists the **Center for Medicare & Medicaid Innovation (CMMI)**, often called the Innovation Center, the key force behind testing and implementing new payment and delivery models. For years, it has been pushing the boundaries of payment reform, often leading the charge where private insurers hesitate but are slowly and reluctantly working to catch up.

While we in the trenches were focused on the immediate encounter — the single office visit, the acute hospitalization — Medicare was looking beyond, taking a broader, more holistic view of patient care.

In recent years, this forward-thinking approach has become even more pronounced. Medicare's focus has shifted dramatically, moving beyond only paying for individual services to a more integrated model that emphasizes episodes of care. This means that instead of simply paying a fee for a doctor's visit or a hospital stay, Medicare is increasingly looking at the entire continuum of care a patient receives for a specific condition — from diagnosis and treatment to recovery and rehabilitation — even after discharge from the hospital.

A common example might be a patient who experiences a hip fracture. An episode of care for this condition would encompass all the services a patient receives from the time they fracture their hip until they are largely recovered. This could include the Emergency Room (ER) visit, the surgery to repair the fracture and related hospital stay, a Skilled Nursing Facility (SNF) stay for rehabilitation and physical therapy, post-surgical follow-up visits, equipment such as a walker or crutches, and any pain management or other necessary prescriptions.

Under an episode-based payment model, all these services — from the initial fracture to the patient's recovery — would be paid under a single bundled payment. This incentivizes providers to coordinate care effectively, avoid duplicative tests or procedures, and focus on the patient's overall recovery. It also encourages them to manage costs, as they are responsible for the total cost of the episode.

Highlighting this point is one of the most expensive orders a physician can ever provide: "Discharge to SNF." That order has historically meant minimal follow-up by the physician until long after the hospital discharge, with the blind expectation that the patient would be well cared for in a different setting — and with the hospital bed now available for the next paying patient. More than likely, the patient was set up for an unnecessarily long and costly SNF stay. While the initial order may be appropriate for continued recovery and rehabilitation, the lack of follow-up can easily spiral downward, often leading to new complications that go unaddressed — further extending the stay or even requiring a new hospitalization for additional surgical or medical interventions.

This shift from fee-for-service (FFS) payment to payment for entire episodes of care has profound implications. It incentivizes collaboration among providers, encourages a focus on preventative care, and ultimately aims to improve patient outcomes while controlling costs. The very system we once derided for its perceived backwardness is now pioneering a path toward a more coordinated system. It's a quiet revolution, happening not in the flash of a new surgical technique, but in the slow, steady evolution of how we pay for and deliver care. And it's a revolution many of us have ignored.

Simply Not Enough

The U.S. nursing shortage has been in the news at varying levels of intensity over the past several decades. Demand for nurses at all licensure levels — from nursing assistants to registered nurses — has consistently outstripped supply. Discussion of the topic prior to the early 2000s often revolved around a lack of nursing graduates, with efforts to address the issue through higher compensation and the recruitment of professionals from foreign countries.

The Philippines has served as the leading source of internationally trained nurses, highly regarded for their education, clinical skills, and English proficiency. India, Canada, South Korea, and, increasingly, Nigeria have also helped fill the nursing gap in the U.S. Nevertheless, the shortage continues as seasoned nurses retire — and as the U.S. population rapidly expands its over-65 demographic, which requires more frequent and complex medical care due to age-related conditions and the increased prevalence of chronic illnesses.

The pipeline of new nurses is simply inadequate. This stark reality was recently underscored during an organization's labor union negotiations, where the union advocated for mandated staffing levels to ensure patient safety and reasonable working conditions. The large, integrated provider organization—made up of hospitals, free-standing emergency rooms, ambulatory surgery centers, and provider clinics — while predictably citing financial constraints, more importantly pointed to the severe lack of available nursing graduates.

Even if the organization were to hire every single graduating nurse from the state's esteemed nursing programs over the next five years—precluding any hiring by competing organizations — the union's proposed staffing levels would remain unattainable. This undeniable fact was ultimately and quietly acknowledged by both parties, leading to the de-emphasis of this particular point in the negotiations.

The healthcare provider shortages are increasingly apparent as the COVID-19 pandemic has intensified the challenges facing the healthcare system — extending the workforce shortfall well beyond nursing staff to include physicians, "mid-level" providers such as Nurse Practitioners (NPs) and Physician Assistants (PAs), and even more entry-level clinical staff such as Medical Assistants (MAs). The pandemic placed immense strain on providers, leading to increased burnout and prompting some to leave the profession altogether. It also disrupted medical education and training, potentially delaying the entry of new providers into the workforce.

The shortages, even for Medical Assistants — who require relatively limited education and practice experience, and whose scope of practice is narrow — are now so severe that generous compensation practices are becoming the norm (compared to just a few years ago). Materially higher salaries, additional perks, and meaningful signing bonuses are now commonplace to attract individuals providing administrative and clinical support to physicians and other healthcare professionals.

Burnout has intensified and further exacerbated shortages at all levels, reaching crisis proportions and threatening not only the well-being of caregivers but also the quality of patient care. The crisis is widely recognized and has even prompted the Surgeon General to publish an advisory outlining steps to address health worker burnout. While acknowledging that the advisory is not intended to be comprehensive, it calls for systemic change—reform of the structures, cultures, and operational norms that shape health care delivery.

As one esteemed national psychiatrist has noted, addressing burnout is a fundamental precondition for delivering exceptional care with genuine compassion. The pressures contributing to this phenomenon are multifaceted and impact healthcare professionals at every level. Caregivers are routinely asked to work excessively long hours, often exceeding what is healthy or sustainable. They face an overwhelming administrative burden that diverts valuable time and energy away from direct patient care. Additionally, many are asked to perform tasks at — or even beyond — the scope of their licensure, adding to their stress and potentially compromising patient safety. Most significantly, they experience a profound and unsustainable emotional toll within the healthcare environment, a burden that was dramatically intensified during the height of the pandemic.

The consequences of this pervasive burnout are far-reaching and deeply troubling. As insiders within the healthcare system, we witness firsthand the devastating impact on our colleagues. Physicians are leaving the practice of medicine, seeking refuge in healthcare administration or exiting the field altogether. Recent conversations with a highly skilled eye surgeon revealed her decision to abandon her practice in pursuit of a more balanced life. Much to everyone's surprise, she is now training on the side and plans to eventually dedicate herself fully to her passion: singing rock and pop music.

Even more tragically, we have witnessed multiple instances of healthcare professionals succumbing to the overwhelming pressures of burnout by taking their own lives. Learning of these deaths of despair — seemingly with no warning signs beyond the intense stress of the profession — is heartbreaking and nearly impossible to bear. These losses represent not only individual tragedies but also a significant depletion of expertise and compassion within the healthcare workforce.

The factors driving this exodus and these devastating outcomes are complex and deeply interwoven. The long hours, administrative overload, and creeping responsibilities contribute to a persistent sense of being overwhelmed and undervalued. The emotional weight of witnessing suffering, making life-altering decisions, and navigating a convoluted, bureaucratic system takes its toll. The pandemic compounded these already existing pressures, pushing healthcare providers to their absolute limits.

We have sorrowfully arrived at a state where the healthcare system risks losing its most asset; the compassionate, dedicated professionals who have the education, experience, and expertise and who have devoted their lives to caring for others. Most troubling of all are the closed-door discussions held by senior leadership executives, who, driven by bottom-line concerns and a lack of empathy for clinical realities, dismissively say, *"Yeah, it's stressful (for clinicians), but that's why they're paid the big bucks."*

Under the current construct, patients face increasing difficulty accessing timely care, leading to delays in diagnosis and treatment. Overworked and stressed providers may be more prone to errors, potentially compromising the quality of care. It can be reasonably argued that the shortages have driven up healthcare costs as demand outpaces supply. And perhaps most concerning of all, underserved communities and rural areas are disproportionately affected, exacerbating existing health disparities and further marginalizing vulnerable populations.

Consolidations

Consolidation in the healthcare industry most often conjures a sense of unease. It's a highly debated topic — a tug-of-war between the promise of efficiency and the fear of diminished patient care. It's still said in close quarters that healthcare is a *"cottage industry,"* with care delivered to individuals at the local level by practitioners, clinics, and hospitals. Centralizing those services is said to improve coordination, offset by the loss of a more personalized connection between patient and provider. The drive for efficiency, cost control, and economies of scale (profitability) has fuelled a relentless wave of consolidation. The landscape is increasingly dominated by large and complex organizations.

One of the persistent — and often frustrating — themes is the pursuit of standardization. The idea that certain processes can be standardized is compelling; from billing to clinical protocols, it's a strategy aimed at reducing costs, improving quality, and ensuring consistency. Indeed, many things *can* be standardized. We can standardize the coding of diagnoses, the administration of certain vaccines, and even some aspects of electronic health records. These standardizations can lead to real improvements in efficiency and data collection.

Yet healthcare is fundamentally human. While some aspects of care lend themselves to standardization, many others simply cannot. Our bodies did not come off an assembly line. Our needs are individual. Chronic conditions and comorbidities are complex, and the critical importance of the patient-provider relationship defies simple formulas. Forcing standardization has led to treating patients as numbers rather than individuals — and simply hasn't worked.

We see giants like UnitedHealthcare acquiring physician practices, entire hospital systems, and, of course, other smaller insurance plans — with some, but mostly little, opposition by regulators tasked with enforcing antitrust laws to prevent monopolies and promote competition. This vertical integration aims to control costs, streamline care delivery, capture market share, improve profitability, and increase publicly traded stock prices. The potential benefits include better care coordination and more efficient resource allocation.

However, concerns arise about reduced competition, which can lead to higher prices and limited patient choice. Furthermore, physician autonomy can be compromised as practices become absorbed into larger corporate structures — moving from ownership to *being owned*. The individual physician, and even small group practices, are becoming more and more like the coelacanth — a truly remarkable fish once thought to have gone extinct millions of years ago, only to be rediscovered in the waters around Madagascar. That is, they still exist — but are critically endangered.

The insurance landscape itself has seen significant consolidation, with mergers creating fewer, larger players. These mergers can increase negotiating power with providers, potentially driving down costs. However, they also raise concerns about market dominance and the potential for anti-competitive behavior. In response — and either as an aggressive or defensive strategy, depending on one's viewpoint — hospitals are merging, physician practices are consolidating, and integrated delivery systems are forming. These strategies allow providers to pool resources, negotiate better rates with insurers, and invest in new technologies.

And the consolidations do not appear to be slowing. Despite expansion through mergers, acquisitions, inflation, and organic growth, the Chief Legal Counsel of a nearly $30 billion, seven-state nonprofit recently suggested, *"We may still not be big enough."*

Navigating the tension between standardization and personalization — ensuring that the drive for efficiency doesn't overshadow the fundamental need for compassionate, individualized care — that's the challenge.

Chapter Eleven: Designing a Better System

Atlantis

The U.S. Space Shuttle program had its share of both praise and criticism. Despite the considerable expense and the technological limitations inherent in freezing designs during construction — resulting in spacecraft that were, in some ways, outdated by the time they launched — the shuttles remain a powerful symbol of human ingenuity and perseverance.

Retired space shuttles can be seen at various locations across the United States. The shuttle that flew the final mission of the Space Shuttle Program, Atlantis (Space Shuttle OV-104), is on display in a cavernous hall at the Kennedy Space Center. Consider the sheer scale: Atlantis—all 122 feet of her, roughly the length of three school buses parked bumper to bumper—contained approximately 2.5 million moving parts. Over the course of 33 missions, she traversed the vast expanse of space, logging 126 million miles. Think about that for a moment. That's like circling the Earth over 5,000 times or journeying to the Moon and back more than 525 times.

While pinpointing an exact number is impossible, the Space Shuttle program was a collaborative masterpiece involving tens of thousands of individuals. Engineers, factory workers, technicians rigorously testing every system, support staff, contractors, subcontractors, NASA employees—all united by a common goal: to succeed.

If we can build a spacecraft capable of traversing millions of miles and supporting human life in the harsh vacuum of space, surely, we can design and implement a healthcare system that serves every citizen of this nation. With a united vision, a collaborative spirit, and the same relentless pursuit of excellence, we can meet the challenge here on Earth. We must merely overcome the lack of will.

Fire station healthcare

A favorite metaphor for thinking about what ails our healthcare system is the local fire department. Think about it: city and county municipalities all around the country fund and support their local fire departments. It's not a short list of large corporations that have been consolidating over time and now have a stranglehold on how fires are fought and put out. They certainly don't make up a sixth of our gross domestic product. Communities fund fire departments and gladly pay for firefighters to sit 24 hours a day, seven days a week — hoping they don't have any fires to put out. Much of the work of local fire departments is being first responders to emergencies, but they also focus heavily on prevention activities such as education, building code inspections, and more. Fire departments have never been embedded within our capitalist economic system — and yet they manage to do many of the things the healthcare industry has failed to do.

Healthcare is big business, and the stakeholders like to use words like "socialized medicine" to stir fear any time we veer a little too close to a government-operated system. That said, how do fire departments do it? How do they successfully save lives and prevent fires from ever starting in the first place? Could it be because they are not financially rewarded for each fire they fight? Is it because they feel personally at risk every time they run toward a fire?

Imagine a healthcare system operating like a fire department. The bulk of the work is in prevention. Caregivers are available for emergencies (access), but most of their energy goes into prevention, safety, and education. In today's healthcare system, we have a lot of fires to put out. Why?

The short answer is this: there is big money to be made solving health problems rather than preventing them — and we are systemically set up to do just that.

So, what do we do about it? We all know we would never intentionally design the system we have today. But what would we replace it with? We don't have the answer to that question yet — but we do believe there is a path to finding it.

The U.S. healthcare system is an ugly collage of big business, political divisiveness, special interests, perverse incentives, and corporate greed.

We've tried to acknowledge the positive attributes, but at the end of the day, it is a systemic failure. Repairing the damage is more unrealistic than replacing it. We need more than just the concept of a plan. We need the stars to align in ways usually reserved for calamitous moments in history — like December 7, 1941, when Japan attacked Pearl Harbor, or the September 11, terrorist attacks.

Overhauling our healthcare system will require a collective willingness to abandon the current paradigm. It will require collaboration and coordination. And most importantly, it will require leadership — perhaps a kind of leadership that does not yet exist. That said, it is not impossible.

What will it take?

We suggest five necessary elements to achieve complete replacement.

ELEMENT ONE:

Common acceptance that the current system has failed.

We can check this one off our list as complete. While there are plenty of defenders of the current state of our healthcare system, those are generally insiders with their own self-serving agendas. As you can see by the most recent Gallup poll on the quality and coverage of healthcare in the U.S., consumers are far from impressed with either.

ELEMENT TWO:

Credible and effective leadership.

The challenge to this element is removing insider agendas and the influence of politics and special interests. Beyond an evolutionary improvement to the current system, what's needed is a revolutionary replacement. And revolutions are rarely led by establishment figures or insiders.

While the current occupant of the White House may like to present himself as an outsider, he is perhaps the most likely president in history to sell out to special interest groups through self-serving transactions with big corporations. Donald Trump will not fix or replace the healthcare system to improve the lives of Americans. At most, he intends to dismantle elements of the Affordable Care Act — ostensibly out of petty revenge aimed at former President Obama.

Leadership must come from outsiders who have a national voice and credibility — not just one individual, but several, and not those looking to build personal wealth or curry favor with special interest groups. Social media has created the rise of "social influencers," and this issue demands a unique kind of influencer: a cross-section of public figures who may differ on nearly every other issue but can find common ground here. Perhaps today's hyper-connected digital world can finally unite us around a topic where nearly everyone agrees: our healthcare system is broken.

With enough momentum rooted in shared acknowledgment of the current state — broken beyond repair — agreement on a viable replacement may emerge through an imaginative collaboration between far-right, far-left, and centrist celebrities, advocates, and policy experts. Could they come together to influence a wide swath of the population and demand revolutionary change? Something better is absolutely possible, but it will require a highly public mandate, transcending social, demographic, and political boundaries.

That may sound like a heavy lift — but consider the precedent. Social media influence has catalyzed some of the most powerful movements of our time: presidential elections, the Arab Spring, WikiLeaks, disaster relief efforts. It's possible.

Most elected leaders in today's U.S. environment rarely lead. Instead, they listen to public sentiment and chase votes. Social media can be the groundswell of demand that force elected leaders to act. Right now, the insiders of the healthcare system — the entrenched stakeholders — still have a choice. That can change. We do not have to accept "no" for an answer.

ELEMENT THREE:

Disabuse stigmatized solutions.

Rather than stigmatizing alternative solutions, brainstorming and evaluating comprehensive alternatives is the order of the day. Let's avoid labeling any public option or a hybrid public option as "socialist". We must also accept that the system will be challenged to perfectly meet the needs and desires of every citizen. Transparency on costs and outcomes performance can give us a stronger system, be it public or private. The old labels and narratives must be eradicated by influencers.

ELEMENT FOUR:

Let real stakeholders design a new system.

While understanding the complexities of delivering healthcare is important, an infusion of our most innovative thinkers and everyday consumers into the design of a new system is essential to any path toward replacement. A robust approach should include a diverse task force — composed of healthcare providers, caregivers, consumers, policy writers, engineers, medical faculty, researchers, and international experts. Their mission: to evaluate what has worked globally, what hasn't, and then to design something entirely new. This ground-up effort should begin with the assumption that nothing currently in place must remain.

After 9/11, it became clear that our national security had been compromised by the siloing of intelligence and law enforcement agencies. In response, the Department of Homeland Security was created, and sweeping reforms were enacted to ensure information could flow across stakeholder groups. One could argue those reforms didn't go far enough — but the urgency and bipartisan response were undeniable.

Responding to the failures of our healthcare system is no less urgent. In fact, it may be even more consequential. A bold, innovative redesign — led by a coalition of those who understand the system and those who experience it — has the potential to save and improve countless lives.

ELEMENT FIVE:

Manage the change.

Change is almost always met with resistance. Fear of what might come next, clinging to what we know — change can shake the best of us. Managed well, change can lead to great things. The internet has changed the way we do everything, some for the better and some arguably not; artificial intelligence promises to test our capacity for change. LGBTQ+ rights have been recognized, along with things

> like marriage equality, to ensure everyone is treated equally. We are a changing society, and our healthcare system is outdated and out of time. Transitioning to a superior U.S. healthcare system that matches or exceeds the performance of other countries — either through legislative means or capitalist incentives — can move our population into a less chaotic, higher-quality, less expensive, and better-coordinated system of care. Accomplishing this will require a clear and transparent transition plan.

Like our local fire departments, our healthcare system should focus more on prevention and education, perhaps more than on fighting fires. The U.S. needs to accept the current state as too broken to be repaired piecemeal, invoke leadership that can influence change, throw away the old and false narratives insiders have used to keep us all from seeing the opportunities clearly, use the best minds and information to design a new system, and create a rational plan to make the transition.

We humbly accept that the fire station metaphor is not perfect. Fires, for the most part, are very different and arguably less complex than the human body, an astonishing ensemble of interconnected systems. Nevertheless, it's reasonable to embrace the ideology of meeting all the population's basic healthcare needs, and even further, to strive to do better — as a wealthy and powerful nation with unimaginable resources and a history of great achievements. While ***We All Die*** is a mere reminder that if you haven't experienced the fragmented and ineffectual U.S. healthcare system yet, your day and our day is coming. It might be time for this cobbled system to die its' own natural death, to be replaced by a system intentionally designed to deliver better care and produce a healthier life for us all.

Epilogue

Let us be clear: We All Die is not leveled at the countless individuals who dedicate their lives, day in and day out, to the noble and often thankless task of caring for the sick and vulnerable. Their commitment, their tireless efforts within a fractured framework, are deeply appreciated and acknowledged. We recognize the inherent good and the honorable intentions within the nationwide network of healthcare professionals, from those at the bedside to administrators behind the scenes.

Furthermore, despite the realities we've shared, we believe there is reason for optimism. We witness the remarkable human capacity for collective action in the face of overwhelming challenges. Communities have rallied and neighbors are helping neighbors to rebuild following the West Coast fire devastations,. Similarly, in the wake of massively destructive natural disasters, we see an innate human drive to alleviate suffering, to feed the hungry in the most challenging of locations.

The enduring commitment of individuals like Chef José Andrés and his organization, World Central Kitchen (WCK), serves as a powerful testament to this spirit. Their long-term, sustainable approach to providing nourishment in times of crisis, evidenced by their staggering achievement of over 450 million meals served worldwide, showcases the profound impact of dedicated action. WCK's work highlights how ingenuity and dedication can bring relief and foster resilience in the face of unbelievable adversity.

Beyond these highly visible efforts, we are certain that a wealth of creative and profoundly intelligent individuals are willing to turn their minds and to dedicate their energy to addressing the healthcare crisis. While We All Die may serve as a stark reminder of the system's failings, it is not intended as a declaration of irreversible doom. Rather, it is a call to action. Just as communities rise from devastation and meals appear in the most unlikely of places, so too can we design and build a healthcare system that truly serves all.

www.ingramcontent.com/pod-product-compliance
Lightning Source LLC
LaVergne TN
LVHW090413210926
848480LV00002B/548
* 9 7 9 8 2 3 1 9 6 4 6 4 2 *